56 ARCHEOLOGY

57 ARCTIC & ANTARCTIC

58 BUILDING

59 PIRATE

60 NORTH AMERICAN INDIAN

61 [W9-DFW-875]

62 OCEAN

63 BATTLE

64 GORILLA, MONKEY & APE

65 MEDIEVAL LIFE

66 FARM

67 SPY

68 RELIGION

69 EAGLE & BIRDS OF PREY

70 WITCHES & MAGIC-MAKERS

71 SPACE EXPLORATION

72 SHIPWRECK

73 CRIME & DETECTION

74 RUSSIA

75 LIGHT

76 ENERGY

77 ELECTRICITY

78 FORCE & MOTION

79 CHEMISTRY

80 MATTER

81 TIME & SPACE

82 ASTRONOMY

83 EARTH

84 LIFE

85 EVOLUTION

86 ECOLOGY

87 HUMAN BODY

88 MEDICINE

89 TECHNOLOGY

90 ELECTRONICS

91 RENAISSANCE

92 IMPRESSIONISM

93 GOYA

94 MANET

95 MONET

96 VAN GOGH

97 WATERCOLOR

98 PERSPECTIVE

99 DANCE

100 FUTURE

101 MYTHOLOGY

102 LEONARDO & HIS TIMES

103 OLYMPICS

104 MEDIA & COMMUNICATION

105 TITANIC

106 FOOTBALL

107 HURRICANE & TORNADO

108 SOCCER

109 PRESIDENTS

110 BASEBALL

DORLING KINDERSLEY **DK** EYEWITNESS BOOKS

RUSSIA

18th-century festive
headdress for a
married woman

Flag of the Russian Soviet Federal
Socialist Republic from 1920 to 1954

Icon of St. Nicholas

Silver samovar for
making tea

Soviet leader
Joseph Stalin

Yury Dolgoruky,
founder of Moscow

Wooden coat of arms
for Russia, 1882

DK EYEWITNESS BOOKS

RUSSIA

Hat pin of
Cossack leader
Bodgdan
Khmelnitsky

Written by
KATHLEEN BERTON MURRELL

Photographed by
ANDY CRAWFORD

Civil War
saber owned
by General
Tulenov

Red Army *shlam* hat

Brightly painted
19th-century
cotton spinner

DK
Dorling Kindersley

Strings of
dried mushrooms

DK
Dorling Kindersley
LONDON, NEW YORK, DELHI,
JOHANNESBURG, MUNICH,
PARIS and SYDNEY

For a full catalog, visit
DK www.dk.com

Project editor Melanie Halton
Art editor Vicky Wharton
Senior managing editor Gillian Denton
Senior managing art editor Julia Harris
Production Lisa Moss
Picture research Monica Allende
DTP designer Nicola Studdart

This Eyewitness ® Book has been conceived by
Dorling Kindersley Limited and Editions Gallimard

© 1998 Dorling Kindersley Limited
This edition © 2000 Dorling Kindersley Limited
First American edition, 1998

Published in the United States by
Dorling Kindersley Publishing, Inc.
95 Madison Avenue
New York, NY 10016
2 4 6 8 10 9 7 5 3 1

Dorling Kindersley books are available at special discounts
for bulk purchases for sales promotions or premiums. Special
editions, including personalized covers, excerpts of existing
guides, and corporate imprints can be created in large
quantities for specific needs. For more information, contact
Special Markets Dept., Dorling Kindersley Publishing, Inc., 95
Madison Ave., New York, NY 10016; Fax: (800) 600-9098

Library of Congress Cataloging-in-Publication Data
Murrell, Kathleen Berton.
Russia / written by Kathleen Berton Murrell.
p. cm. — (Eyewitness Books; v. 74) Includes index.
Summary: An overview of the land, people, history, and
culture of Russia from its earliest days to the present.
1. Russia — History — Juvenile literature. 2. Soviet Union —
History — Juvenile literature 3. Russia (Federation) —
History — 1991 — Juvenile literature.
[1. Russia — History. 2. Soviet Union — History. 3. Russia
(Federation) History.] I. Title.
DK41.M965 2000 947 — dc21 97–38878
ISBN 0-7894-5881-0 (pb) ISBN 0-7894-5880-2 (hc)

Color reproduction by Colourscan, Singapore
Printed in China by Toppan Printing Co. (Shenzhen) Ltd.

Alexander Pushkin's
silver tea strainer

16th–17th
century Russian
pole ax

Nikolai Gogol's
feather quill

Wooden
gingerbread
mold

Catherine the
Great's ivory
hunting gun

Cross-country
skis and poles

Early 19th-century Russian ice skates

Contents

Vladimir Lenin's
funeral train

Early Russia

MODERN RUSSIANS ORIGINATE from the eastern Slavs who settled in the steppelands of European Russia in the 6th century. In the 9th century Vikings, *Varangians*, sailed from the Baltic Sea along the Dnieper River to establish the trade route from Scandinavia to Byzantium. One of their chieftains, Rurik, founded the first dynasty of Russian princes, and his successor, Oleg, established Kievan Rus, the first Russian state. Catastrophe struck in 1237 when Tatar (Mongol) forces raided many Russian cities, which then remained under Tatar rule for 200 years. Russia was split into many small principalities, one of which, Moscow, gradually gained power and broke the Tatar control.

LARGE AND WEALTHY
Prince Oleg founded Kievan Rus in the 9th century. For 400 years it was one of the largest and richest states in Europe under great rulers such as Vladimir I, Yaroslav the Wise, and Vladimir Monomakh. But in 1237 Kiev, weakened by internal feuding, was destroyed by the Mongol forces (Golden Horde) of Batu, grandson of Genghis Khan.

Kievan 12th-century gold enamel pendants were used to adorn headdresses

RURIK THE VIKING CHIEFTAIN
The *Varangians* were Norsemen, or Vikings, who in the 9th century penetrated from the Baltic Sea into the land of the eastern Slavs, attracted by the trade route between Scandinavia and Greek Byzantium. The Slavs, plagued by enemies and internal feuds, invited the *Varangians* to come and rule over them. One of the *Varangian* chieftains, Rurik, took up the challenge to become prince of Novgorod in 862. The few Norsemen were soon absorbed by the Slavs and the House of Rurik reigned until the end of the 16th century.

FROM KIEV TO MUSCOVY
At its peak, in 1054, the Kievan state stretched from the Black Sea to the Baltic Sea, and north to Lake Onega. After the decline of Kiev, Russia's center moved northeast, first to Vladimir and then to Moscow, capital of the principality of Muscovy. Muscovy included lands as far north as the White Sea and east beyond the Volga, to western Siberia.

RULER OF THE MONGOLS
From his base in Asia, the remarkable Mongol leader Genghis Khan conquered China, northern India, what is now Pakistan, and Central Asia. Later, in 1222, he swept into southern Russia with his brilliant mounted troops, plundering the land between the Volga and Dnieper rivers. His grandson, Batu, completed the domination of Russia in 1237, taking most of Kievan Rus and the newer towns of Vladimir and Suzdal before riding west to conquer Hungary and Poland.

Armor for a
14th–15th century
Mongol warrior

*These flexible
plates protect the
neck and allow
easy movement*

THE GOLDEN HORDE
The followers of Genghis Khan and his grandson,
Batu, were skilled horsemen and archers well
protected by impressive armor. Batu established
the headquarters of his state, the Golden Horde,
at Sarai at the mouth of the Volga. The Mongol
overlords did not attempt to colonize the Russian
principalities but kept control with frequent raids
and by demanding heavy annual payments.
Although the Orthodox Church was tolerated
by the Mongols, their 200-year rule severely
retarded the development of Russian
cultural and social life.

*Leather straps
fasten the upper
part of the suit*

*Ribbon of
St. Andrew was
the highest award
in tsarist Russia*

FIGHTING THE TATARS
Moscow gradually became the center of
opposition to the Tatars (Mongols). In
1380 the Moscow prince Dmitry defeated
the Tatars on the River Don, and in 1480
another Moscow prince, Ivan III, tore up
the document demanding tributes. But it
was not until the 16th century that Russian
forces, under Ivan the Terrible, succeeded
in recapturing land from the Tatars.

*Scepter that was
originally held
by the eagle on
this wooden coat
of arms of 1882
has long since
disappeared*

*Double-headed
eagle holds orb,
a symbol of
state power*

COAT OF ARMS
The double-headed eagle, a
popular symbol of state power
in Byzantium and Europe, was
also adopted in 15th-century Muscovy,
together with the figure of St. George
slaying a dragon. In 1672 the state coat of
arms was declared to be the double-headed
eagle wearing three crowns and holding
the orb and scepter, with St. George on a
shield at the center, surrounded by the
arms of major towns and Siberia. Later the
arms of Finland, Poland, Georgia, and
Taurida (Crimea) were added, together
with the ribbon of St. Andrew.

*The flexible armor
came below the knee
for maximum
protection*

*Mongols relied
on their accuracy
with bow and
arrow to bring
down the enemy*

*Mongol warriors
slashed with the sword
during close encounters*

*St. George
and the dragon*

A varied land

RUSSIA IS THE LARGEST country in the world, straddling the two continents of Europe and Asia and crossing 11 time zones. Its three geographical regions are European Russia in the west, up to the low-lying Ural Mountains; the huge, flat expanse of Siberia; and the mountainous far eastern region. The climate is extreme – average temperatures range from -4°F (-20°C) in winter to 68°F (+20°C) in summer. Russia's mighty rivers include the Volga, Europe's longest river, and the Yenisei in Siberia. Huge Lake Baikal in eastern Siberia is the deepest in the world and contains one fifth of the world's fresh water. Russia's rich variety of animal life includes tigers, reindeer, moose, sable, walrus, and the unique Baikal seal.

Reins attached to these notches are used to steer the sleigh

SOLITARY TIGER
The magnificent Siberian tiger, the largest tiger in the world, lives in solitude in the forests and mountains of the far eastern Ussuri region. Although the number of Siberian tigers fell disastrously to about 20 in the 1940s, a policy of protection has ensured their survival. By the mid-1990s, about 300 were known to exist.

Traditionally drawn by three horses, a Russian sleigh is often called a troika, from the Russian for "three"

Curved front shields passengers from spray kicked up by the horses

SYMBOL OF A NATION
The common brown bear, one of the national symbols of Russia, lives in the mountains and forests of the entire country from Europe to Siberia and the mountains of the Ussuri region, in the far east. Such large creatures can sustain themselves in semihibernation throughout the winter on the fruits and berries of the forests; on fish; and even on deer which they can bring down by covering short distances at enormous speed.

Animal furs make snug blankets for passengers

IN A COLD CLIMATE
Surprisingly, Russia's severe climate has not impeded winter travel, for roads of packed snow are smoother than the ruts of summer or the muddy tracks of spring and autumn. Horse-drawn sleighs, such as this one, can travel rapidly over snowy highways while passengers recline snugly under the furs. In the past, when sleighs traveled long distances, horses were changed at government post stations, placed at regular intervals along the main routes. Although most sleighs have now been replaced by cars and trucks, they are still used in some rural areas.

Step enables passengers to climb into and out of the sleigh easily

SIBERIAN SURVIVAL
This ivory carving shows how the reindeer makes it possible for people to live in the isolated parts of northern Siberia. Indigenous (native) peoples, such as the Chukchi, rely on domesticated reindeer herds to provide transportation, meat, milk, and hides for clothing and tents.

VEGETATION ZONES
Russia can be divided into broad horizontal bands of vegetation: the treeless tundra in the north, which widens eastward to include the far eastern region; the taiga, the great forests that dominate most of Russia; and the steppes, or meadowlands, in the south.

TUNDRA SUMMER
In June and July the warm sun thaws the Arctic soil a few inches down to the permafrost, permanently frozen earth over 0.62 miles (1 km) thick. During this time, the normally bleak landscape is briefly transformed by brightly colored flowers and green grasses.

TAIGA FORESTS
The great taiga forests of larch, pine, spruce, birch, and aspen account for over half of the world's resources of softwood and provide habitats for many of Russia's wide variety of animal species.

GRASSY PLAINS
Steppes, or treeless grasslands, are distinguished by a thick layer of extremely fertile black earth that is ideal for agriculture. The steppes are found in the southern parts of European Russia and Siberia.

In Verkhoyansk, the coldest inhabited place in the world, temperatures can drop to -96°F (-71°C)

Arctic Ocean

Kamchatka Peninsula

•Moscow

Don

Ural Mountains

Yenisei

Volga

Ob

Lena

Siberia

Russian Federation

Lake Baikal

Vladivostok•

☐ Steppe
▧ Taiga
☐ Tundra

Cushioned backrest provides comfort on long journeys

Handle is gripped by the coachman when the sleigh is in motion

Coachman sits on leather stool during journey

Coat of arms indicates that this sleigh belonged to an important family

These shoe-shaped leather footrests protect the coachman's feet from the harsh elements

Metal blades stabilize the sleigh as it glides over ice

FRIEND OR FOE?
The villain of Russian fairy tales, the large gray wolf is now found only in the wilds of Siberia and the remoter areas of European Russia. With its thick fur, which whitens the farther north it travels, it adapts admirably to life in a cold climate. Its poor reputation is undeserved, for although it will kill sheep and farm animals when in desperate hunger, attacks on human beings are very rare.

Distinctive black-and-white wing markings

RED-BREASTED GOOSE
Black, white, and chestnut red, these most vivid of all geese breed in the far northern reaches of Siberia, bordering on the Arctic Ocean. These beautiful birds are living proof that the huge, almost uninhabited regions of Russia's cold north can support a colorful variety of life during the warmer months of the year, June to August. But the number of breeding pairs has declined by over two thirds in the past century, mostly because of indiscriminate hunting.

Peoples of Russia

BEFORE THE REVOLUTION, Russia was a truly multiethnic empire, which included Ukrainians and Belorussians; Kazakhs and other peoples of Central Asia; Georgians, Armenians, and Azerbaijanis in the Caucasus region; Lithuanians, Latvians, and Estonians in the north; Tatars; Germans; and many others. Even present-day Russia, which is much smaller, has over 100 nationalities among its 150 million people. But ethnically "Russian" Russians are the vast majority, at 82 percent of the population. Just over half the Soviet Union's people were Russian, and in the Russian empire Russians were a minority.

Soft swansdown pom-pom

COSSACKS
Russians largely made up the Cossack (p. 23) self-governing communities in the Kuban, Astrakhan, and Orenburg provinces in the south. However, some Cossack settlements were not Russian but Kalmyk and Buryat (Mongol peoples), Bashkir (Turkic-speaking), and Tungus (native Siberian).

KOKOSHNIK
Red velvet hats with gold embroidery, like this one, were Russian women's everyday wear for centuries. All but the highest nobility wore the *kokoshnik*.

FAMILY HEIRLOOM
This festive 19th-century outfit with its delightful pom-pom hat comes from the Ryazan area, south of Moscow. The owner would have made the blouse, skirt, apron, and sleeveless jacket herself. She would have spun the linen thread from flax, then woven the material and sewn the clothes together. Finally she would have done all the embroidery and crochetwork. Such a fine outfit would have been handed down within the family.

Ryazan designs are typically geometric

Apron displays fine crochetwork

NATIONAL DRESS
Along with the *kokoshnik*, Russian peasant and servant women all over the country wore a sleeveless dress (*sarafan*) until the 20th century. The decoration and color of the *sarafan* differed greatly from district to district.

REPUBLIC OF TATARSTAN
Turkic-speaking Tatars form about 4 percent of the population of Russia – about 6 million people. Most live in the Republic of Tatarstan within the Russian Federation. They are descendants of the Golden Horde (p. 11) and many of them are Muslims. In 1994 Tatarstan signed a treaty giving it special rights within the Federation.

Hooded costume of Tatar women reflects the now rare custom of veil wearing

Hood prevents loss of body heat and keeps head and ears warm in sub-zero temperatures

Tungus nomad

Tungus town dweller

Men of Tobolsk

NATIVES OF SIBERIA
Today Russians greatly outnumber the many small groups of indigenous (native) Siberian peoples. The two native Siberians (above right) are from the Tobolsk area, west of the Urals. Those on the left are Tungus from the Amur district on the border of China. The one in the long fur-lined coat is a town dweller and next to him is a nomad, who lives with his reindeer herds.

Mittens are sewn into the sleeves to keep out biting winds

THE NORTHERN PEOPLE
This warm coat comes from the Nganasan people, the most northerly inhabitants of Russia, whose way of life resembles that of the Inuit. There are only a few thousand Nganasan; they belong to the Samoyed-Nenets group and live on the Taimyr Peninsula in northern Siberia. They lived traditionally as nomadic hunters, reindeer herders, and fishermen, although in the Soviet period many were forced to settle on collective farms.

Wealth of a nation

RUSSIA HAS VAST reserves of natural resources, from timber – about one fifth of all the world's forests – to a remarkable supply of rocks and minerals. These include huge deposits of gold, diamonds, iron ore, copper, nickel, lead, and zinc. There are also large deposits of fossil fuels including coal – half the world's reserves – oil, peat, and natural gas. Fur trapping, Russia's earliest source of wealth, is still practiced. Fishing, particularly for sturgeon, is a highly developed industry, and Russia's long rivers are used to generate over 10 percent of the world's hydroelectric power.

Polished amber bead

Crystallized gold nugget

DIAMOND DISCOVERY
Until the 19th century diamonds, such as those in the imperial crown, above, were imported from India. Russian diamonds were first discovered in 1955 in an isolated spot in north central Siberia. Within a year a new town, Mirny, had been built. It has good links by air, but the nearest railroad is over 600 miles (1,000 km) away. However, Mirny is now a town of about 40,000 people, who are mostly involved in diamond production.

ANCIENT AMBER
Amber is fossil resin – a thick, sticky substance from extinct conifers. It is found mostly along the Baltic Sea; for thousands of years, people have polished it, traded with it, and made it into jewelry. The Catherine Palace (p. 29) had a famous room lined with panels of amber.

MINING FOR MINERALS
Iron ore and other metals are especially abundant in Siberia. The northern Siberian town of Norilsk (p. 39), beyond the Arctic Circle, was founded in the 1930s to extract rich deposits of nickel, copper, and cobalt, and now also produces gold, silver, and platinum.

GOLD RUSH
Russia has some of the largest gold reserves in the world. In 1838 a discovery near the Yenisei River in Siberia, followed by huge finds near the upper Lena River, started a gold rush. In 1923 another major find was made at Aldan on the upper Lena.

Russian nobleman in fur-lined coat and fur hat

Furry side flaps untie to cover ears in especially cold weather

Front flap folds down to cover forehead

FUR TRAPPING
To combat the harsh cold of winter, most Russians wear fur hats and coats with the fur on the inside. Animals are still trapped extensively in the wild, mostly by native peoples. There are also many fur farms where mink, sable, and fox are raised for their skins. But the fur of animals living in the wild is considered the best.

FUR TRADERS
Early traders from central Russia headed north and east in search of the pelts of animals from the Russian Arctic. By the 17th century fur was the most important item of foreign trade for the merchants of Moscow. The annual fur auction in St. Petersburg is still considered the most important fur market in the world.

Deep green with pale green streaks, malachite is a popular stone for carving into objects, such as this 19th-century vase from Yekaterinburg in the Urals

NATURAL GAS
The leading producer of fossil fuels, Russia has 40 percent of the world's natural gas. Deposits lie in the northern Caucasus, Siberia, and along the Arctic coast. Pipelines laid in the 1970s and 1980s, linking the Siberian gas fields with European Russia, made it much easier to export the gas to other countries. Those exports help pay for imports.

Laying pipelines in northern Russia is difficult and expensive because of permafrost (p. 11)

MIGHTY STURGEON
As the Volga and the Caspian Sea become polluted, the huge sturgeon that provide caviar (fish eggs), an expensive luxury dish, are becoming scarce. Nevertheless, fishing is a major industry in Russia. Russia's modern fishing fleet works both in coastal waters and out on the open seas of the Atlantic and Pacific.

Arms move up and down as if washing the bear in the tub

MALACHITE
This beautiful green copper compound occurs in only four places in the world, including the Ural Mountains of Russia. In the 19th century, malachite was used to make jewelry, furniture, and beautiful objects, such as this vase, for high society. The interior walls of the Malachite Hall in the Winter Palace (p. 28), a room for ceremonial occasions, are completely lined with the bright green stone.

Traditional Russian toy carved from wood

HYDROELECTRICITY
With its immense rivers, Russia has built many dams to generate electricity. Stalin favored huge hydroelectric projects, such as reversing the flow of rivers, but recently these have been rejected because they would damage the environment.

TIMBER
Russia has about one fifth of the world's forests and nearly half the world's softwood (pine and other conifers). Siberian forests are remote, so tree felling is concentrated nearer to markets in central Russia and the Urals. The wood is used to make paper, furniture, and village houses, and much is still used as firewood.

A life of serfdom

SERFS WERE PEASANTS bound to their landlord's estates and forced to work the land. They were virtually slaves, for they could do nothing without their lord's approval – not even marry. They could be bought and sold, exiled to Siberia, or forced to join the army. But the law forbade landlords to kill their serfs. Until the 17th century, on one day each year, serfs were allowed to move to another estate. In 1649, even this freedom was abolished. Two centuries later, in 1861, serfs were finally freed. The liberated serfs provided labor for new industry, which led to spectacular economic growth. But peasants were charged high prices for the land they believed was theirs by right; freedom brought little improvement to their lives.

THE ARISTOCRATS
Until the end of the 17th century, the aristocracy shared the same culture, language, and religion as the peasants. But as Peter the Great (pp. 20, 22) forced the nobles to shave their beards and adopt Western dress, customs, and languages, the gap between aristocrats and peasants widened immensely.

ESSENTIAL TOOLS
Peasants on Russia's large estates continued to use wooden agricultural implements, scarcely improved since medieval times, until well into the 20th century. Most landlords, with unlimited cheap peasant labor, did little to improve the land or farming methods. But some, such as the writer Tolstoy, supported more progressive farming techniques.

LOG HOUSES
Villages with identical log houses, called *izbas*, are still common all over Russia, although straw roofs are now rare. The *izba* has one large room for the extended family, dominated by a great stove that is also used as a warm sleeping bench during the long winters.

CAPTURE OF PUGACHEV
Runaway serfs fled to the borderlands in the south and became Cossacks, or free warriors, farming and organizing their communities far from the heavy hand of the tsar. In 1773 Yemelyan Pugachev, a Cossack leader, declared himself Emperor Peter III, murdered husband of Catherine the Great. Promising liberation of the serfs, he led a popular revolt of peasants of Russian and other nationalities in the Volga and Ural regions. He was at first successful, capturing Kazan and threatening Moscow, but was defeated at Tsaritsyn in August 1774. Pugachev escaped, but was captured in December and brought to Moscow in this specially built cage, and publicly tortured and executed.

Flail was used to beat crops to separate the grain from the husks and stalks

Hand-crafted rake used for gathering hay and smoothing soil

Wooden handle

Free-swinging wooden bar

Pick has sharp metal head for breaking up clumps of soil and stones

Peasants carried their lunch and personal belongings in bags woven from birch bark

PEASANT LIFE
Before the Revolution of 1917, four out of five persons in Russia were peasants. Only one fifth were literate, but they were skillful craftspeople, able to construct their own houses, spin cloth, and make all their own agricultural tools. Peasants belonged to a tight-knit village commune, or *mir*, whose elders were responsible for collecting taxes, settling disputes, and allocating land.

Loose linen blouse with lace-up collar kept peasants cool on hot summer days

Brightly colored wool skirts were spun at home

The sickle's curved blade is used to cut grass and crops, such as wheat

Female serfs often wore many layers of skirts to keep them warm in the winter

FREEDOM TO THE PEOPLE
In March 1861, serfs celebrated throughout Russia as news spread of Tsar Alexander II's emancipation law. About 50 million Russian people were thus freed from near slavery. However, the former serfs were still bound to their commune and in debt for what little land they received. Many felt cheated and remained dissatisfied with their situation.

Traditional serfs' shoes, called lapti, *were hand-woven from birch bark*

TRADITIONAL ATTIRE
Women's everyday wear was a simple blouse and skirt, or a sleeveless dress, called a *sarafan*. Men wore trousers, linen shirts, and a caftan. In summer peasants wore birch-bark shoes. In winter they put on felt boots, or *valenki*, and sheepskin overcoats with the fur on the inside, to keep themselves warm in the snow. More elaborate costumes were kept for special occasions and handed down from generation to generation.

17

Orthodox religion

Aʟᴛʜᴏᴜɢʜ ᴍᴀɴʏ ʀᴇʟɪɢɪᴏɴs, including Buddhism and Islam, are found in Russia, most of the population identifies with Orthodox Christianity. Adopted from Byzantium over 1,000 years ago by Prince Vladimir, it was chosen for the splendor of its ceremonies. Rich in ritual, Orthodox services are often long, elaborate, and colorful. Priests chant and the choir sings without the accompaniment of musical instruments, because it is believed that only the human voice should be used in sacred music. Orthodoxy remained Russia's State religion until the Revolution in 1917. In the Soviet era many churches were destroyed; priests were shot or imprisoned. Since 1990, when official support was renewed, the Church has rapidly revived.

WEDDING CEREMONY
During an Orthodox marriage service, ornate crowns, like the poet Pushkin's, above, are held over the heads of the bride and groom. The couple drink wine three times from the same cup. The priest then leads the couple three times around the center of the church.

Slanted bar on Russian Orthodox cross represents where Christ's feet were nailed

St. Nicholas, the 4th-century Byzantine bishop

Embossed metal covers this icon, revealing only the hand and face of the painted saint

NIKON'S REFORMS
Patriarch Nikon was head of the Church from 1652 to 1658. His reforms to rituals, such as making the sign of the cross with three fingers instead of two, met with strenuous opposition from a group called the Old Believers, who separated from the Church. When Nikon tried to make the Church more powerful than the State, the tsar imprisoned him in a remote monastery.

SACRED PICTURES
Sculptures were discouraged by the Church for a long time because it was thought that they might become objects of worship. But icons – religious pictures painted on wooden panels – could be venerated (deeply respected) because they are not lifelike images. Icons are found not only in churches, but also in Russian homes.

MONASTERIES
Although most of the ancient monasteries were forced to close after the Bolshevik Revolution and were neglected or destroyed, many have been vigorously revived in the new Russia. The most important is the beautiful Trinity Lavra of St. Sergius, founded in the 14th century. In 1689, its enterprising monks supported Peter the Great in his struggle for the throne against his half-sister, Sophia.

Oil lamp for lighting up icons

Apostle Matthew

Apostle John

Angel tells Mary she will bear the son of God

Apostle Luke

Apostle Mark

ROYAL DOORS
The royal doors are at the center of the iconostasis – the tall wall of tiered, religious paintings that screens the altar from the rest of the church. The congregation stands throughout the service, facing the iconostasis. Only the clergy are permitted to enter through the royal doors, which are opened at certain moments during services, symbolically revealing heaven to the faithful.

CHURCH CLERGY
At the head of the Church is the patriarch. He, like all senior ranks of the Orthodox Church – the metropolitans, archbishops, bishops, and archimandrites – is drawn from the unmarried "black" clergy (monks). The more numerous priests, the "white" clergy, are normally married and often remain parish priests all their lives. Women are not permitted to enter the clergy.

Orthodox bishop

Golden chalice

Bishop's miter

Miter is a symbol of a bishop's power

Elaborately bound Book of the Gospels

HOLY BOOK
The Bible was translated into Old Church Slavonic in the 9th century by Saints Cyril and Methodius. Church Slavonic is close to the Russian language and is still used today in church services.

The stole, omoforion, is only worn by bishops

Girdle

Cuffs are laced around the wrist

The palitza, which hangs from the right hip, is worn by bishops and some senior priests

The sacchos hangs down to the mid-calf

The sacchos, or bishop's vestment, symbolizes the robe of Christ

Staff, or crosier, signifies that the bishop is a shepherd of his people

CEREMONIAL ROBES
The robes for ceremonial occasions in the Orthodox Church are often magnificent and richly colored, like these bishop's vestments. Each item of clothing has a special religious significance. Both bishops and priests normally wear a black cassock, or robe, and a black hat (*skufya*). For services, priests have their own special vestments, many of which are similar to those of the bishop. More ornate robes are worn by bishops and priests for Easter and other important festivals.

Priestly stole, epitrachelion, hangs down almost to the floor

Rule of the tsars

RUSSIA HAS KNOWN two royal dynasties: the Rurikids (c. 860–1598) and, following the Time of Troubles (c. 1605–13), the Romanovs (1613–1917). The chaotic Time of Troubles was a period of civil strife when many imposters fought for the throne, and unrest, famine, and invasion plagued the country. Russian princes adopted the title "tsar" from the Roman "Caesar" in the 15th century, as the power and prestige of Moscow grew. The title "emperor" came into use in the 18th century under Peter the Great. Tsars throughout Russian history ruled with absolute power.

THE ROMANOV DYNASTY
In 1613, 16-year-old Mikhail Romanov was elected to the throne. His family continued to rule for the next 300 years. The dynasty ended in February 1917 when Nicholas II abdicated (gave up the throne).

Gold crown studded with pearls, garnets, and turquoise

Sable-fur trimming made crown more comfortable to wear

CROWN OF KAZAN
Thought to have belonged to Ediger Mahmet, this 16th-century crown is one of the oldest in Russia. Mahmet was the last ruler of the Tatar state of Kazan. He adopted Christianity and became loyal to Ivan the Terrible.

IVAN THE TERRIBLE
Ivan IV's long rule (1533–1584) began hopefully, with new laws, territorial conquests, and commercial relations with England. After the death of his first wife, however, Ivan began a reign of terror, even murdering his own son.

Peter and Paul Fortress in St. Petersburg, painted 1723

Porcelain frame decorated with enamel on copper

BORIS GODUNOV
Unpopular Boris Godunov ruled at the end of the Rurikid dynasty. He was suspected of murdering the rightful heir, Prince Dmitry. Godunov died suddenly in 1605, resulting in a prolonged battle for a successor. The Time of Troubles had begun.

PETER THE GREAT
Peter I, who took the throne by force from his half-sister, Sophia, ruled from 1689 to 1725. The most energetic of the tsars, he founded a new capital city (pp. 28–29), established the navy (p. 22), initiated radical reforms in education and government, and was the first tsar to travel abroad.

CATHERINE II
Born a German princess, Catherine became empress of Russia in 1762 and ruled for over 30 years. Known as Catherine the Great, she was the last of four strong empresses to rule after Peter I.

DECEMBRIST REVOLT
Throughout Russian history, there were many peasant uprisings against tsarist rule. But the 1825 revolt against Nicholas I by the aristocratic Decembrists shocked the regime. With little support, the revolt soon died out. Five of the leaders were hanged and the rest condemned to hard labor in Siberia.

Executed leaders of the Decembrist Revolt

Ring made from chains that bound Decembrists in Siberia

Cupid holds the orb and scepter, which are symbols of state power

TSARS' SECRET POLICE
The notorious secret police of the tsars, the Third Department (later the Okhrana) infiltrated and suppressed revolutionary organizations. But the organization's cruelty pales beside the brutality of the Soviet secret police, the NKVD (later the KGB).

Empress Elizabeth's monogram

Carved and gilded female head

Like all Russian tsars, Alexander II was an accomplished horseman

Imperial coat of arms – St. George and the double-headed eagle

ALEXANDER II
The highlight of Alexander's reign was the emancipation of the serfs in 1861. But the reforming tsar was killed by a terrorist's bomb in 1881. His successor, Alexander III, pursued harsh, reactionary policies, reversing many of his father's reforms.

Nicholas and Alexandra wear 17th-century tsarist costumes for a grand ball, 1903

Golden embroidery on red velvet

STRONG EMPRESSES, WEAK EMPERORS
After the death of Peter I in 1725, the rest of the 18th century was dominated by strong empresses, among them Peter I's daughter, Elizabeth, and German-born Catherine II. Assisted by elite guards, each took the throne by force from weak emperors, and both enjoyed the popularity of the general public. The ornate decoration of Elizabeth's gilded throne (above) is typical of her extravagant taste. Both Elizabeth and Catherine were responsible for most of the opulent palaces and royal estates in and around St. Petersburg.

LAST IN LINE
Nicholas II celebrated the 300th anniversary of the Romanov dynasty in 1913. Four years later, however, he abdicated on behalf of himself and his hemophilic son following the catastrophe of war and civil rioting. The tsar and his family were murdered by the Bolsheviks in 1918 (p.32).

Empire building

THE HISTORY OF Russia is one of almost continual expansion. It has been estimated that from 1600 to 1900 Russia grew at a rate of 50 square miles (130 square km) a day! With no natural barriers to the east or west, Russia lay open to repeated invasions throughout its history. After gaining strength, Russia expanded its frontiers, partly to protect its vulnerable heartland. By the end of the 18th century, Russia included Siberia, western Ukraine, Lithuania, Poland, and Tatar Crimea. In 1809, Finland was added, and in the first half of the 19th century, the small countries of the Caucasus – Georgia, Armenia, and Azerbaijan – and huge areas of Central Asia became part of the empire.

FOUNDER OF THE RUSSIAN FLEET
Peter the Great, the first tsar to interest himself in naval matters, founded the Russian fleet after studying shipbuilding in Holland and England. In the Great Northern War with Sweden (1700–21) he expanded Russian territory to the Baltic Sea, gaining Swedish territory in southern Finland, the marshes on which he built his new capital, St. Petersburg, and what are now Estonia and Latvia. Peter the Great also captured the long peninsula of Kamchatka and the Kurile Islands in the Pacific Ocean.

Hatpin of Ukrainian Cossack leader Bogdan Khmelnitsky

Brass gun barrel

Porcelain cup showing General Bagration

Type of cannon employed at the Battle of Borodino

BAGRATION AT BORODINO
Leading a French army half a million strong, Napoleon invaded Russia in June 1812. By September, he had succeeded in reaching Borodino on the approaches to Moscow. A bloody battle broke out in which many were mortally wounded, including one of the most brilliant commanders of the Russian army, a Georgian prince, Pyotr Bagration. Afterward, the Russians, led by the crafty, one-eyed Marshal Mikhail Kutuzov, retreated. Napoleon took Moscow but was driven out in October.

Wooden wheels are strengthened with metal

IMPERIAL EMPIRE

By 1914 the Russian empire was by far the largest in the world, stretching from the Arctic Ocean to the Caspian Sea and from the Baltic Sea to the Pacific. Within its borders were diverse nationalities ranging from the northern ice-bound Chukchi to the desert nomads of Kazakhstan. The huge empire, which included Finland and Poland, was divided into provinces and ruled from St. Petersburg.

Defense of Sevastopol 1854–55

CRIMEAN WAR

In the Crimean War (1853–56), Russia fought against Britain, France, and Turkey. Russia, badly led and poorly supplied, was defeated despite the heroic year-long defense of Sevastopol, on the Black Sea, and a naval victory against Turkey. Under the peace treaty, Russia kept the Crimea, but its power in the Black Sea was weakened.

EXPLORING ALASKA

Fur-rich Alaska, separated from Siberia by narrow straits, was first visited by Russians in 1741. In 1789 Joseph Billings, an English sailor in Russian service, led a secret expedition to study Alaska's peoples and explore its coast. The United States bought Alaska in 1867.

Letter of July 1791 carved on walrus tusk, and sent to Billings from Siberia, documents landings on Alaskan coast

RUNAWAY SERFS

The first Cossacks were runaway serfs and outlaws who formed frontier settlements in southern Russia and Ukraine. At first, Cossacks opposed the Russian authorities, but by the 19th century they had turned their settlements into prosperous agricultural communities and were fiercely loyal to the tsar.

Cossack shashka sword

CONQUEST OF SIBERIA

Ivan the Terrible opened the way to the resources of Siberia when he defeated the Tatars at Kazan on the Volga. Yermak, a daring Cossack leader, penetrated farther into fur-rich western Siberia in 1581, as shown in Surikov's painting of 1895. With 840 men he conquered the native tribes and greatly expanded Russia's borders.

Cannons were dragged to their battle positions by horses

MILITARY COSSACKS

Cossacks wore distinctive uniforms, with tall fur hats and sheepskin cloaks; they carried a sword (like this *shashka*, right) and a long lance. All Cossack men had to serve in Cossack military units, which were famous for their loyalty, bravery, and fine horsemanship.

DEFEAT OF NAPOLEON

In 1812, the French took Moscow. But a terrible fire destroyed most of the city, including winter supplies. After just a month Napoleon, the conqueror of Europe and Egypt, was forced to retreat. Frozen and starving, 90 percent of his men died or deserted. Two years later, the Russians, under Alexander I, rode triumphantly into Paris and Russia began to play a prominent role in European affairs.

Life at court

I N MUSCOVITE TIMES (pp. 8–9) the royal court was at the Kremlin in Moscow. Tsars were attended by bearded *boyars* (nobles), wearing ornate costumes. Elaborate court rituals, such as the deep kowtow (bow), were based on Byzantine customs and those of the former Mongol overlords. The imperial court at St. Petersburg (1712–1917) adopted Western dress and manners, imitating French King Louis XIV's opulent court of Versailles. The Russian emperor or empress was attended by French-speaking aristocrats.

Scepter is decorated with the Orlov diamond, one of the largest in the world

SILVER SPECTACLES
Catherine the Great was a prodigious reader, correspondent, and writer of plays. She used these elegant spectacles (with their enamel case) when working at her desk.

CROWN JEWELS
The diamond-studded Grand Imperial Crown of 1762, made for Catherine II's enthronement, was used in all subsequent coronations. The central band of diamond oak leaves and acorns, symbols of state power, begins with Empress Elizabeth's perfect diamond of 56 carats and ends with a magnificent Chinese ruby of nearly 400 carats.

Gilt cupids adorn the front of the carriage

CORONATION CEREMONY
The crowning of Nicholas II in 1896, shown above, took place at the Assumption Cathedral, Moscow. Coronations continued to be held in the cathedral after the capital moved to St. Petersburg. Nicholas II's coronation celebrations were horribly marred when 1,200 peasants were killed in a stampede of people waiting to receive royal gifts.

GRAND PALACE BALLS
From the elegant dances held by Alexander I to the sumptuous fancy-dress affairs of the fun-loving Elizabeth, lavish balls were the highlight of the winter season in St. Petersburg. Olga, Nicholas II's eldest daughter, made her debut in 1913 at the last glittering ball held before the Bolshevik Revolution.

Two or three pairs of matched horses would have drawn the carriage

Wooden wheels with metal rims

IVORY HUNTING GUN

Hunting was a favorite pastime of the court. The fine workmanship of Empress Catherine's gun, made in about 1780 at Tula, south of Moscow, is typical of the skill of Russian craftsmen. There is a famous legend that when English smiths gave Nicholas I a miniature dancing steel flea, the expert Tula craftsmen responded by fitting it with tiny boots.

Steel barrel

Flintlock mechanism

Gold-embossed ivory grip

Emperor Paul

FANCIFUL FABERGÉ

Peter Carl Fabergé, a St. Petersburg jeweler of French origin, made spectacular and intricate ornaments. Every year Nicholas II ordered Easter eggs for his wife and mother. This egg, with 18 miniature portraits of the tsars, was made in 1913 to celebrate the Romanov dynasty.

Peter the Great

Nicholas II

Elegant wooden canopy decorated with gilt laurel and oak leaves

Coachman sits on velvet-draped box while controlling the horses

Carved golden eagle acts as a guardian

System of leather straps supports the body of the carriage

Scenes of cupids and goddesses are painted on the side panels

Back wheels are larger than front wheels for easy turning

CATHERINE'S CARRIAGE

Catherine the Great's lover, Count Grigory Orlov, organized the coup against her husband. He presented the empress with this ornate summer carriage, made of gilded wood and painted with scenes on the paneled back and sides. On ceremonial occasions elegant horse-drawn carriages would fill the streets leading to the Winter Palace or the Kremlin in seemingly endless processions.

City of domes

Central octagonal tower is topped by a small gold cupola

AFTER THE TATARS' DEFEAT in 1380, Moscow gained in power and, by the 15th century, had become the leading city of Russia. Although Peter the Great moved the capital to St. Petersburg in 1712, Moscow, the "second capital," still played a major role. In 1812 Napoleon captured Moscow. But the city was soon ablaze – probably set on fire deliberately by its citizens, who preferred to flee rather than surrender. Napoleon's starving army, faced with the onset of winter, was then forced to retreat. The rebuilt city prospered, and became the capital again in 1918, under the Bolsheviks. Before the October Revolution, Moscow was known for its amazing domed churches, but half were destroyed during the Soviet era. In the new Russia, many are being rebuilt.

CITY FOUNDER
Moscow was founded by Prince Yury Dolgoruky. It is first mentioned in early Russian chronicles in 1147, when Dolgoruky invited other princes to a feast. The first wooden fortress was built in 1156, on the hill where the Kremlin now stands.

Kremlin W *Red Square*

CITY BOUNDARIES
This 1605 map shows how Moscow developed in a circular pattern. Expanding eastward from the Kremlin to embrace Red Square, the city then widened in a walled horseshoe around the original core. Wooden palisades (fences) and dirt ramparts (embankments) were built in 1592 to circle the whole wooden town. This old town center now makes up only 2 percent of the modern city.

ST. BASIL'S CATHEDRAL
Dominating Red Square is the fantastic Cathedral of the Intercession, better known as St. Basil's. It is named after a holy man who dared to stand up to Ivan the Terrible. The cathedral was built between 1555 and 1561 to celebrate Ivan's victory over the Tatars. It consists of eight chapels topped by ornate domes grouped around the central church tower. Ivan allegedly blinded the architects to ensure that this masterpiece could never be rivaled.

All Saints Gate guarding the bridge across the Moscow River

Ivan Veliky bell tower, for many years the tallest building in Moscow

Medieval palaces, including the tsars' Terem Palace

All Saints, or Great Stone, Bridge, built in 1692

VIEW OF THE KREMLIN
The Kremlin, the high-walled triangular fortress on the Moscow River, shines with 33 golden domes and contains the great cathedrals and former palaces of the tsars. Italian Renaissance architects built the walls and most of the churches between 1475 and 1505. After the 1917 Revolution, Lenin, and then Stalin, lived and worked in the Kremlin. Today it houses the office of the Russian president.

Onion domes

Cupolas, or domes, first appeared in the north of Russia. The familiar onion shape may have developed because it sheds snow more easily than the shallow Byzantine dome from which it was adapted.

An early helmet-shaped dome

Highly decorated gables

King post would have supported a tall wooden cross

Scarf joint bonds the two king posts for maximum strength

Church of the Intercession, Rubtsovo, 1626

Church of St. Nicholas, Bersenevka, 1657

INTO THE DOME
Pine wood, readily available in northern Russia, was easily shaped by skillful axmen to make the dome. Supported by the king post and spindle beams, three-piece struts were slotted together; nails were not used. The framework was then linked with cross boarding to mold the frame. Wedged outer shingles were of moist aspen, which gives a silvery glow.

KIZHI ISLAND CHURCH
The ultimate in northern wooden architecture is the Church of the Transfiguration, built in 1714. Its 22 cupolas rise in elaborate tiers to form a striking silhouette. In the flat landscape these cupolas resemble the pine trees of the surrounding forests.

Wedges ensure sufficient tension

Spindle beams, like spokes in a wheel, provide horizontal support to the frame

The middle strut makes the bend necessary for the onion shape

Three-piece struts – 16 in all – run from the drum to the top post

St. Basil's in Red Square peeps over the Kremlin

Beklemishev Tower defended the eastern approaches on the Moscow River

Overlapping tongued shingles, lemekhi, are made of aspen wood

Cross boarding links the vertical struts forming the frame

Drum, or base, of cupola

27

Palaces of St. Petersburg

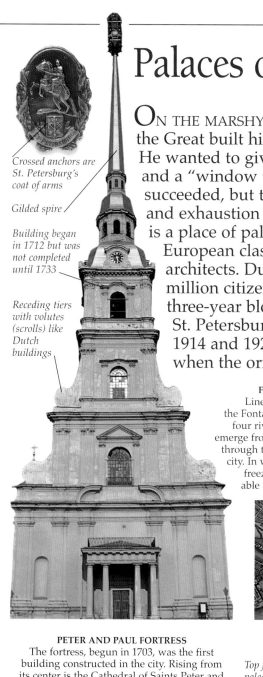

Crossed anchors are St. Petersburg's coat of arms

Gilded spire

Building began in 1712 but was not completed until 1733

Receding tiers with volutes (scrolls) like Dutch buildings

ON THE MARSHY banks of the River Neva, Peter the Great built his new capital, St. Petersburg. He wanted to give Russia an outlet to the sea and a "window to the west." By 1712 he had succeeded, but thousands had died of fevers and exhaustion in the process. St. Petersburg is a place of palaces and spires, reflecting the European classical style of its many foreign architects. During World War II over a million citizens died as a result of a nearly three-year blockade by the German army. St. Petersburg became Petrograd between 1914 and 1924, then Leningrad until 1991, when the original name was restored.

Alexander Column is a memorial to the 1812 victory over Napoleon

THE ARCHITECT RASTRELLI
The Italian Bartolomeo Rastrelli (1700–71) was court architect under Empresses Anna and Elizabeth. He built stunning royal palaces of astonishing size and color, with lavish interiors. But his work fell out of favor with Catherine II, who preferred classical architecture.

FROZEN FONTANKA
Lined by grand houses, the Fontanka River is one of four rivers and canals that emerge from the Neva to loop through the center of the old city. In winter the Fontanka freezes so hard that it is able to support vehicles.

CITY LAYOUT
St. Petersburg is grouped around narrow rivers and canals with the broad Neva River at the center. Large islands like the Vasilievsky on the left and Hare Island, where the fortress stands, face the mainland. Nevsky Prospekt is the most important of the streets that radiate from the Neva River.

PETER AND PAUL FORTRESS
The fortress, begun in 1703, was the first building constructed in the city. Rising from its center is the Cathedral of Saints Peter and Paul. With its tall, slim spire, it symbolizes the city as much as St. Basil's does Moscow.

Top floor of the palace was used as servants' quarters

WINTER PALACE
The magnificent Winter Palace, begun in 1754 for Empress Elizabeth and completed in 1762, is Rastrelli's crowning achievement. It is a closed square with a spacious courtyard built on the banks of the Neva River. It burned down in 1837 but within a year was rebuilt almost exactly as before. Long the main residence of the tsars, the Winter Palace became the Hermitage Museum after the Revolution.

Ornate cupolas can be seen from a considerable distance

GRAND INTERIORS
Rich interiors like this palatial dining room are often found in 18th- and 19th-century palaces, not only of the tsars but also of high-ranking members of the aristocracy. Marble columns are used in abundance in halls based on Greek and Roman architecture. Precious materials such as amber decorate the walls, and gold leaf is found everywhere.

Elaborate window frames are typical of Rastrelli

CATHERINE PALACE
These gold cupolas belong to the chapel of the Catherine Palace. This royal summer residence stands at Tsarskoe Selo, on the outskirts of St. Petersburg. It was designed by Rastrelli for Empress Elizabeth and named after her mother. The palace's landscaped gardens were laid out during the reign of Catherine the Great.

SMOLNY CONVENT
Rastrelli was responsible for Empress Elizabeth's Convent of the Resurrection. Its first ornate buildings were completed in 1764, after Elizabeth's death. In contrast to the extravagant exterior, the interior was left undecorated. Catherine II confiscated the convent to use it for Russia's first girls' school, whose students were young noblewomen. The school later became the headquarters of Lenin's Bolsheviks; here he planned the October 1917 Revolution.

Gilt Peterhof statue

PETERHOF
Peterhof, on the Gulf of Finland, was Peter the Great's favorite summer residence. The palace, modeled on the French palace and gardens at Versailles, was begun in 1714 and was later added to by Rastrelli. The Grand Cascade of fountains was adorned with many gilded statues. The palace and grounds were ruined during World War II but have been beautifully restored.

Grand Cascade of fountains

Gold cupola pinpoints position of the palace cathedral

Catherine II's rooms were on the second floor, in the southeast corner

Bolshevik Revolution

AFTER RIOTS in Petrograd (St. Petersburg until 1914) in February 1917, Nicholas II abdicated the throne and a Provisional Government took over. The Revolution had many causes. In 1905, widespread discontent erupted in strikes, uprisings, and mutinies. Food shortages, the tsar's weak leadership, and Russia's disastrous performance in World War I heightened unrest. Failure to stop the war angered soldiers and peasants, and in October 1917 the Bolshevik (Communist) Party, led by Vladimir Lenin, seized power. Lenin dissolved the Provisional Government and made peace with Germany at the cost of huge territories, including Ukraine.

GRIGORI RASPUTIN
The fake holy man Grigori Rasputin gained huge influence over Nicholas II and Empress Alexandra because of his apparent ability to cure the hemophilia attacks of their son and heir, Alexei. While the tsar was at the front during World War I, Rasputin virtually ruled Russia. In 1916 the unpopular Rasputin was murdered by relatives of the tsar.

Peaceful demonstrators slain by tsar's troops

WORKERS UNITE
In Moscow, the 1917 Revolution was very violent compared to the almost bloodless coup in Petrograd. Militant workers fought fiercely against the stronger forces of cadets loyal to the Provisional Government. Only after ten days of furious fighting around the Kremlin did the Bolsheviks emerge triumphant in Russia's second capital.

Blank shots fired from the Aurora *signaled the start of the Bolshevik uprising*

"BLOODY SUNDAY"
On January 9, 1905, a young priest, Father Gapon, led workers from St. Petersburg's factories to the Winter Palace to petition the tsar. Hundreds of peaceful demonstrators, including women and children, were killed when soldiers opened fire. The massacre shook the nation's faith in the tsar.

WWI Russian troops wear gas masks while fighting in the trenches

WORLD WAR I
Russia, an ally of France and Britain, entered World War I in 1914. Russia's troops fought bravely and at first won important victories against Austria and Germany. But her armies lacked adequate supplies and later suffered defeats, with heavy casualties and desertions. Popular enthusiasm gave way to disillusion and war-weariness.

SIGNAL FOR THE REVOLUTION
The sailors of the cruiser *Aurora* mutinied against their officers in March 1917 and joined the Bolsheviks. Anchored on the River Neva in central Petrograd, the *Aurora* fired a blank shot on October 25, 1917. The shot signaled the storming of the almost undefended Winter Palace, where the remaining members of the Provisional Government were meeting.

LEON TROTSKY
The dynamic revolutionary Leon Trotsky was imprisoned and then banished for his part in the 1905 Revolution. He escaped abroad and joined the Bolsheviks in 1917. Trotsky was the main organizer, with Lenin, of the October Revolution. He became commissar (head) of foreign affairs, and then of war, and went on to organize and lead the Red Army during the Civil War.

Official stamp making document legal

Membership number

Issued to Comrade Andrei Andreev

Joined the Party on September 2, 1912

Member was most likely exempt from monthly payments since none are logged

COMMUNIST PARTY MEMBERSHIP
Lenin's party was known as the Social Democratic Labor Party until 1919, when it was renamed the Communist Party. Its members were called Bolsheviks. This membership ticket belonged to Andrei Andreev, who joined the Party in 1912. He was a member of its top policy-making committee, the Politburo, from 1932 to 1952. He was one of the few Old Bolsheviks to survive Stalin's purges (pp. 35, 36).

BOLSHEVIK LEADER
Vladimir Lenin, a revolutionary since student days, was banished to Siberia in 1897. He believed that workers had to rebel against the establishment to create a fair society. In 1900 Lenin went abroad, where he began a ruthless campaign to gain total control of the exiled Russian Social Democratic Labor Party. The party split: Lenin's group, the "Bolsheviks" (majority), opposed the "Mensheviks" (minority). In 1917 Lenin returned to Russia to lead the Bolshevik Revolution.

TOPPLING OF THE TSARS
Many tsarist symbols were destroyed after the Bolshevik Revolution. Nicholas II's huge statue of his father, Alexander III, was toppled in 1918. Lenin, who ordered it to be destroyed, never forgot that his elder brother had been executed for plotting to assassinate Tsar Alexander.

Medal marks the 15th anniversary of the Revolution

PETROGRAD GUARDS
The Red Guards were armed units, mostly of factory workers, who played a key part in seizing power for the Bolsheviks. This medal was awarded to Red Guards who defended Petrograd during the Revolution and Civil War (pp. 32–33).

The Civil War

THE COMPARATIVELY bloodless October Revolution (pp. 30–31) was followed by a cruel civil war between the anti-Communist White Army and the Bolshevik Red Army. The White forces lacked strong leadership but, aided by Western powers, enjoyed early successes. In 1920, however, the Red Army, joined by many tsarist officers, was victorious. Although the Bolsheviks lost Poland, Finland, and the Baltic states, the rest of the Russian empire remained within the new Communist state. The horror of civil war was followed by a terrible famine, relieved only by U.S. aid. In 1921, to restore the ruined country, Lenin announced the New Economic Policy. This reintroduced private trade.

WAR BOATS
River steamers like this one, rechristened *Vanya the Communist,* were taken over for use in the Civil War. The boat was destroyed in a fierce battle on the River Kama in October 1918.

Shield protects machine-gun operator from enemy bullets

Machine gun mounted on a former private carriage

Imperial sword

Execution of Tsar Nicholas II

SLAUGHTER OF THE ROMANOVS
In July 1918, the White forces threatened Yekaterinburg in Siberia, where the Bolsheviks were holding Nicholas II, the former tsar. Early on July 17, 1918, by Lenin's order, the tsar and his family were murdered. Their bodies, burned and buried in a pit in the forest, were not discovered until 1992.

ПРОЛЕТАРІЙ ВСЕХ СТРАН СОЕДИНЯЙТЕС'! В БОРЬБЕ ОБРЕТЕШ ТЫ ПРАВО СВОЕ!

"Workers of all countries unite! In struggle you will win justice!"

WORDS OF MARX
This Bolshevik banner quotes the words of Karl Marx, who, in his *Communist Manifesto* (statement of aims), urged the workers to unite since they had nothing to lose but their chains. After the October Revolution, however, power went not to the workers but to the Communist Party leaders.

Tsarist Imperial Army badge

WHITES AGAINST REDS
White Army soldiers were against the Communist takeover for a variety of reasons: some still supported the tsarist regime; some wanted the Provisional Government (p. 30) to be restored; while others were completely opposed to Bolshevik ideas.

RED ARMY TROOPS
The ill-disciplined voluntary Red Guards were transformed into the Red Army by the brilliant commander Leon Trotsky. He appointed former tsarist officers and reintroduced order and distinctions between officers and soldiers. He kept close contact with the army by traveling quickly to areas of conflict in his armored train.

Red Army cap badge, 1919

Flaps can be turned down to keep ears warm in winter

ARMY RECRUITMENT
Mass conscription (the draft) meant that many army recruits came straight from the countryside with little or no military training. They were reluctant soldiers: many deserted the army and returned to their villages, especially at harvest time.

"I am a plowman on guard, with my rifle I stand, I preserve freedom and my land"

ВСЕОБЩЕЕ ВОЕННОЕ ОБУЧЕНИЕ – ЗАЛОГ СВОБОДЫ

Я ПАХАРЬ НА СТРАЖЕ С ВИНТОВКОЙ СТОЮ ХРАНЮ Я СВОБОДУ И ЗЕМЛЮ СВОЮ.

DRESSED TO KILL
Red Army uniforms were haphazard affairs. Many soldiers wore their own clothes, or captured White uniforms, and crude birch-bark *lapti* shoes instead of boots. The pointed hat with the star, called a *budyonovka* after Marshal Budyonny, came to symbolize the Red Army soldier.

Sight aligns eye with target

MARSHAL BUDYONNY
This pistol belonged to Red Army commander Marshal Budyonny, a former officer in the Imperial Cavalry. His skilled horsemanship in battle became legendary.

Order of the Red Banner, 1921

RED COMMISSAR
Commissars were Party members attached to Red Army units to ensure political loyalty. They carried arms and were better dressed than most army members.

Seat for soldiers

Document case for paperwork

Carriage was drawn by horses

CIVIL WAR CARRIAGE
The *tachanka*, a horse-drawn carriage with mounted machine gun, is typical of the makeshift methods of the chaotic Civil War. This *tachanka* was employed in a famous battle in which Germans, Poles, and Ukrainian nationalists fought for control of the Ukraine before the Reds finally won in 1920.

Metal-rimmed wooden wheels made it difficult to maneuver the carriage on rough terrain

The rise of Stalin

WHEN LENIN DIED IN 1924, the struggle was on to inherit the leadership of the Communist Party. Trotsky, the most able candidate, was soon outmaneuvered by Joseph Stalin, the devious secretary general of the Party. Stalin joined with two other leaders to defeat Trotsky, then formed a new alliance to oust them as well. Trotsky was exiled in 1929. Stalin then strengthened his power by launching rapid industrialization and agricultural collectivization. The Great Terror began in earnest with the murder in 1934 of the leading Bolshevik, Sergei Kirov. The secret police, the NKVD (later the KGB), became all-powerful, directing mass arrests from their infamous headquarters in Moscow. All the famous Old Bolshevik leaders were tried or shot.

DESTRUCTION OF CHURCHES
Churches were not only closed but, by the late 1920s, began to be destroyed in large numbers. The massive Cathedral of Christ the Savior (p. 58) in Moscow was completed in 1883 as a memorial to the Russian victory over Napoleon. It was blown up in a huge explosion in 1931 to make way for the Palace of the Soviets (see below).

Train was made at the Putilov factory in St. Petersburg, 1910

Renovated in 1923, the train became a memorial to Lenin in 1937

This 1920s cartoon reflects Lenin's wish to convert the world to Communism

LENIN'S FUNERAL TRAIN
When Lenin died in January 1924, his body was brought to Moscow by train for a huge public funeral. His body was embalmed (preserved) and placed in a specially built mausoleum (tomb) in Red Square, where you can still see it today. The mausoleum also served as a platform for Soviet leaders viewing the annual parades on May Day and November 7 (pp. 56–57).

Р.У. Ж.Д. У. 127

LENIN AND WORLD REVOLUTION
This cartoon of Lenin sweeping the world clean of priests, capitalists, and kings illustrates the Communist hope that the Revolution would spread around the world. But Communism was not successful abroad. At home Lenin persecuted merchants, monarchists, and priests, closed churches, and nationalized trade and industry.

MONUMENTAL PALACE
This design for the Palace of the Soviets was drawn in the 1930s. It was to be the tallest building in the world. But only the foundations were laid since building problems and World War II halted construction.

Motherhood award could be attached to a chain and worn proudly as a necklace

MOTHERHOOD AWARDS
After the Bolshevik Revolution, the government supported women's freedom, but by the 1930s traditional roles of women as wives and mothers were emphasized. To encourage a higher birthrate, the Motherhood Medal was granted to women with five children; those producing ten were declared Heroine Mothers.

RULE OF STALIN
Joseph Stalin became leader after Lenin's death by outmaneuvering Trotsky, Lenin's natural successor, and other leaders. In the late 1920s he introduced forced collectivization of agriculture and rapid industrialization, which brought many hardships. Freedom of thought in the arts was also suppressed. Any remaining opposition was eliminated in the mass purges of 1937 (p. 36).

Hammer and sickle were adopted as emblems of the new state

COLLECTIVE FARMING
Collective farms combined small holdings into single units, often including several villages. Despite the invitation on this poster, peasants had no choice. In 1929 Stalin launched forced collectivization. The peasants resisted and millions died, or were shot or sent to labor camps. Production fell, causing a terrible famine. By 1938 collectivization had spread throughout the Soviet Union.

"Come to us in the collective farm!"

Stalin's real name was Dzhugashvili. Stalin comes from "stal," the Russian for steel; he adopted the name while he was working secretly for the early Bolsheviks

Soviet children were cared for in state crèches while their mothers worked

WOMEN'S ROLE
The new Soviet state granted women full legal equality. But by the 1930s the state became more authoritarian and women were expected to perform a dual role. They not only had to cook, clean, and shop for the family, but also do heavy manual labor on the farms or in the new factories. Childcare was organized to release women for work outside the home, but poor housing and lack of amenities made their lives arduous.

Stalin's mustache, simple clothes, and high leather boots were copied by the other leaders

35

Soviet Russia

GERMAN INVASION
Breaking the Nazi-Soviet peace pact, Germany invaded the Soviet Union in June 1941. Stalin and the Red Army were taken by surprise and much of the western Soviet Union was occupied. But the Germans were turned back from Moscow, defeated at Stalingrad on the Volga in 1943, and pushed back to Berlin. They finally surrendered at Reims, France, on May 7, 1945. Two days later, Red Army soldiers gathered in front of the mausoleum in Red Square, Moscow, and threw captured Nazi flags before Stalin and other leaders.

DURING STALIN'S PURGES millions of innocent people were executed or sent to remote labor camps (*gulags*). These horrors were followed by the hardships of World War II. When the Soviet Union was invaded, Moscow nearly fell to the Germans and Leningrad suffered a long siege. After the war, good relations with Western allies deteriorated and the Cold War began. After Stalin's death in 1953, relations began to improve. But in 1962, Khrushchev built missile launch sites in Cuba, which led to a showdown with the U.S. Finally, after Gorbachev became Party leader in 1985 and introduced the policies of *glasnost* (freer speech) and *perestroika* (reform), the U.S.S.R. and the West grew friendly.

Dzherzhinsky, founder of the Cheka, *the Soviet secret police*

Mass grave marking from a gulag *near Karaganda in Central Asia*

LABOR CAMPS
Wooden grave tablets recorded only the burial sites – no prisoner names or numbers – of those who died in Stalin's labor camps (*gulags*). An estimated 20 million people were swallowed up in the huge concentration camp system.

STATE UNIVERSITY
The old Moscow University was expanded in Soviet times, and a large new university building was erected in the Lenin Hills. The building is one of Stalin's seven ornate, tiered skyscrapers, which changed the face of Moscow in the early 1950s. They are popularly known as wedding-cake palaces.

Constructed 1949–53, the central tower is 36 stories high

The vast building contains not only departments and lecture halls but living quarters for the staff and students

Building's lower wings extend out from the center in U shapes

FOUNDER OF THE SECRET POLICE
Felix Dzerzhinsky was the first head of the Soviet secret police, then called the *Cheka*, after the 1917 Revolution. His hated statue (above), which stood on Lubyanka Square opposite the KGB headquarters in Moscow, was pulled down after the failed coup of 1991 (pp. 58–59). It now stands in a sculpture park in Moscow, along with statues of other leaders of the rejected Soviet regime.

CUBAN MISSILE CRISIS
In 1962, during the long Cold War (period of hostility between western countries and the Soviet Union), Soviet leader Nikita Khrushchev placed missiles in Cuba, within range of U.S. cities. Cuba, a Communist state ruled by Fidel Castro, was a strong supporter of the Soviet Union. U.S. President John F. Kennedy immediately ordered a naval blockade of Cuba. Six days later Khrushchev backed down; the missiles were removed. War had barely been avoided. The Communist Party's Central Committee forced Khrushchev to retire in 1964.

CONTROLLING THE ARTS
Under Stalin, writing, art, and even music had to praise Communism, Soviet life, and Stalin himself. *Worker and Peasant*, a sculpture by Vera Mukhina, was made for an exhibition in Paris in 1937.

Worker and Peasant, *"looking into the glorious Communist future,"* was the symbol of Mosfilm, the large U.S.S.R. film studio

Sickle symbolizes the agricultural worker

Hammer signifies the factory worker

SOVIET SYMBOLS
Favorite themes for Soviet emblems were sheaves of wheat and the hammer and sickle used to decorate railings on one of Moscow's bridges. Portraits of the Party leader, hung on the walls of every office and institution, were changed when that leader fell out of favor. Instead of advertising, huge Party slogans decorated city streets and buildings.

The figures, made of stainless-steel panels, are young, strong, and attractive

Anniversary meeting of the Bolshevik Revolution took place here in 1941, as bombs fell outside during World War II

MOSCOW METRO
The construction of the Moscow subway was one of the engineering feats of the Stalin era. Its ornate stations were referred to as "palaces for the people." The first line opened in 1935 and each marble-lined station was decorated with sculptures or mosaics displaying a different theme. Most large cities in Russia now have a metro system. One of the most beautiful stations is Mayakovskaya (above).

Rail and industry

ALTHOUGH A LATE starter, by 1914 Russia had become the fifth largest industrial power in the world. After the Revolution and Civil War, production of manufactured goods fell sharply but rose again when Stalin launched his Five-Year Plans. However, tight government control left little room for new ideas, and Soviet Russia fell behind other modern economies. Industry was in crisis when the Soviet Union broke up in 1991, and production fell further when the new government moved abruptly to a market economy. In such a large country, the railroad network is vital. The first line, from Tsarskoe Selo to St. Petersburg, opened in 1837. By 1899 it had been extended east, greatly helping to open up the vast mineral wealth of Siberia.

"...TO WORK, COMRADES!"
Propaganda posters called on people to throw themselves into the work of the new factories. In 1929 Stalin's first Five-Year Plan was approved, under which rapid expansion of heavy industry was to be achieved by setting monthly and annual targets. In spite of tremendous hardships, by 1937 the Soviet Union had become the second largest industrial nation in the world.

COLLECTIVE FARMING
Industry was utilized to manufacture mineral fertilizers and farm machinery to meet the needs of the new collective and state farms. Traditional wooden farming implements (pp.16–17) were cast aside in favor of modern machinery.

Early Soviet tractors ran on diesel and were deliberately large for the enormous fields

Powerful lights enabled farmers to work through the night

Only the first tractors were fitted with wheel studs; later ones used caterpillar treads

FIRST SOVIET TRACTOR
This is the first tractor to roll off the production line of the Soviet Union's first tractor factory, which opened in 1930. Farm machinery was not kept on farms but at district "machine and tractor stations" (MTS's), which decided when and where they would be used. Until they were scrapped in 1957, MTS's kept the farms under tight political control.

Built in 1956, this was the last Soviet steam train

PASSENGER TRAINS

Russian trains are all electrified or use diesel engines. They have a wider gauge (track width) than European trains; the carriages – especially the sleeping cars – are more spacious, but cause problems at border crossings where the undercarriages have to be changed. There are no rapid trains as in Europe. The 404-mile (650-km) journey from Moscow to St. Petersburg takes five hours by express train.

LAYING THE TRACKS
Russia's first railroads were laid by thousands of workers using little more than pickaxes. During World War I, German prisoners of war built the important line to the ice-free port of Murmansk, above the Arctic Circle. The new line in eastern Siberia, the Baikal-Amur Magistral (BAM), completed in the 1980s, was built largely by volunteers from the *Komsomol* (Communist youth group).

RAILS ON PERMAFROST
It is very difficult to lay railroad lines in northern and eastern Russia, where the layer of permafrost (p. 11) can be almost 3,300 feet (1 km) thick and the earth is unstable during the short summer thaw. Nevertheless, rails have been successfully built beyond the Arctic Circle. They range as far as the coal-mining settlement at Vorkuta and the copper and nickel mines at Norilsk, where Stalin's concentration camps supplied forced labor from the 1930s to the 1950s.

TRANS-SIBERIAN RAILWAY
At 5,777 miles (9,297 km) the Trans-Siberian is the longest railroad line in the world. It runs from Moscow through Siberia to the Pacific, with spur lines to Mongolia and China. Building began in 1891 and was finally completed in 1916. Workers had to overcome terrible problems of terrain and climate as they laid tracks through forest and around the southern edge of huge Lake Baikal. The journey, which lasts 11 days, brings home to travelers the enormous expanse of Russia.

УЛААНБААТАР — МОСКВА

The Soviet T-34 was regarded as the best tank of World War II

Tank is painted white for camouflage in the snow

MASS-PRODUCED WEAPONS
At the start of World War II, hundreds of factories were moved east to the Urals and Siberia, beyond the reach of the invading German army. Tractor factories were adapted to produce tanks, including the T-34, which played a big part in Russia's victory. After the war, Soviet industry continued to mass-produce weapons – over 20 percent of the country's budget was spent on defense. In the new Russia, military spending has declined.

Kapitza's lenses

Science pioneers

RUSSIA HAS A LONG record of outstanding scientific achievement. In the 19th century Russian scientists made important advances in chemistry, radiotelegraphy, and mathematics. In the Soviet era, military science and space technology had priority, but political interference and unjustified arrests of scientists stifled progress. In 1980 Andrei Sakharov, whose theories enabled the Soviets to build a hydrogen bomb, was exiled for defending human rights. Russia was first to send an artificial satellite, and then a person, into space.

FATHER OF AVIATION
Nikolai Zhukovsky (1847–1921) is often called the father of Russian aviation. In the early days of flying he pioneered the study of aerodynamics. In 1905, he figured out how to calculate the lifting power of an airplane; later, he developed the whirlwind theory, on which helicopter flight is based.

Living quarters on this model spaceship are above – control rooms below

Distillation jar used in experiments by Lomonosov

ATOMIC THEORIST
Mikhail Lomonosov (1711–65) was the greatest scientist of his day. A pioneering chemist and physicist, he anticipated part of the atomic theory two centuries before it was fully described. He was also a poet and a founder of Moscow University.

PAVLOV'S SALIVATING DOGS
As a physiologist, Ivan Pavlov (1849–1936) studied the brain, the nervous system, and digestion. By repeatedly sounding a bell at meal times, he trained a dog to salivate at the sound of the bell, rather than at the arrival of food. Through this study, Pavlov developed the theory of conditioned reflexes, which he later applied to humans. He won a Nobel Prize in 1904.

Metal filings in the coherer detect electrical waves and send signals via wires to coils

FIRST RUSSIAN RADIO
Alexander Popov (1859–1905), a physicist, invented the antenna (aerial). In 1895 he made his first radio, right, on which a message could be sent via an antenna to a receiver. The protoype still works. The invention greatly improved communications between ship and shore and assisted in the development of the telephone. Also, telegrams could now be sent by radio waves instead of over cables. The Italian physicist Guglielmo Marconi, who knew of Popov's experiments, patented a radio at about the same time.

Electrical coils connect to a large battery at the back

VISIONS OF SPACE TRAVEL
Konstantin Tsiolkovsky (1857–1935), a schoolteacher, was regarded as a dreamer for imagining space travel nearly a century before it happened. In 1903 Tsiolkovsky designed this spaceship and correctly wrote the theory of rocket power. In the 1920s, Tsiolkovsky developed the idea of jet engines, and proposed that rockets propelled by liquid fuel could be used to send ships into space. But the technology that would make space travel a reality was not available during his lifetime.

Bell sounds when tapped by the stimulated electrical coils

KAPITZA'S PHYSICS

Pyotr Kapitza (1894–1984) won a Nobel Prize in 1978 for his work on low-temperature physics. Kapitza worked in England in the 1920s and 1930s. On a visit home in 1934, Stalin made him stay in the Soviet Union. From 1946 until Stalin's death, Kapitza was under house arrest for refusing to work on the atomic bomb. But he kept up his research using handmade apparatus.

Cartoon of Kapitza, 1971

This tiny thermos could hold liquid helium at the low temperatures needed for Kapitza's research

Four extendable aerials protrude from aluminum sphere

Aluminum sphere contains a radio transmitter

Balloon basket in which Mendeleyev watched an eclipse of the sun

SOVIET SATELLITE

On October 4, 1957, to the astonishment of the world, the Soviet Union launched Sputnik I. Designed by the brilliant rocket and engine scientists Sergei Korolev and Valentin Glushko, Sputnik was the first artificial satellite; it made one full orbit of the earth. The Space Age had begun; ultimately people landed on the moon, and unmanned probes reached Mars, Venus, and Jupiter.

MENDELEYEV'S BALLOON

Dmitry Mendeleyev (1834–1907) was an unusual combination of a great scientist and a successful businessman. He drew up the periodic table of chemical elements, fundamental to the study of chemistry. He also did pioneering work in crystallography and on petroleum, gases, and liquids. Among his main interests were meteorology and astronomy. When an eclipse of the sun occurred over Russia in 1887, Mendeleyev went up alone in this balloon basket to closely observe and take notes on the phenomenon.

FIRST IN SPACE

Only four years after the launch of Sputnik I, the Russian Yuri Gagarin (1934–68) became the first person in space. On April 12, 1961, he was launched into orbit aboard the capsule Vostok I, and made one circuit of the globe in 1 hour and 48 minutes before ejecting from the capsule and returning to earth by parachute. Gagarin died a few years later, when his jet plane crashed during a training flight.

41

Media and communications

Contemporary Russian uses the Cyrillic alphabet, which was developed in the 9th century to provide a written language for Slavic people. Largely based on the Greek script, Cyrillic also shares many letters with the Latin alphabet. The first Russian book was printed in 1563. Shortly afterward, moralizing tales in comic-strip form (*lubok*) were printed. These were the earliest form of popular newspapers; they remained popular until the 19th century. At the beginning of the 20th century, as more people learned to read, regular newspapers became common and book publication greatly expanded. Soviet Russia made great efforts to develop radio, cinema, and television – partly because of their value in spreading state propaganda.

POSTAL SYSTEM
Russia had a primitive postal system as early as the 13th century. By the 17th century the mail was better organized, with post stations providing fresh horses at stages along major routes. In 1874 Russia joined the International Postal Union. The modern system serves the whole vast country using air, rail, and water transport.

Although buried for centuries, the writing is still legible

Birch bark is flattened for ease of writing

BIRCH-BARK TABLET
By the 13th century the northern city-state of Novgorod enjoyed a high standard of literacy, and even a form of democracy. Paper was not yet in common use, so messages were sent on pieces of birch bark, such as this one which conveys greetings to a citizen of Novgorod. These ancient letters were dug up by archaeologists from the University of Moscow in 1960.

Amplifier for broadcasting sound

Large wooden box containing receiver circuits

CYRILLIC SCRIPT
The Russian alphabet is known as Cyrillic after St. Cyril. He and his brother, St. Methodius, adapted the Greek alphabet in the 9th century to provide a written language for Slavic people. Cyrillic's 33 letters match all the vowels and consonants used in Russian speech. This means the language is written just as it is spoken and is very easy to spell and pronounce correctly.

PROMOTING LITERACY
Before the reforms of Alexander II (p. 17), most Russians could not read or write. The opening of new schools meant that by 1917 over 40 percent of the nation was literate. This poster was part of the Bolshevik campaign of the 1920s to achieve 100 percent literacy.

GOING TO PRINT
Ivan Fyodorov, who printed the first Russian book in 1563, was run out of Moscow by the scribes, who were afraid of losing their jobs. In the early years of the 20th century, as people became more literate, a great expansion took place in book and newspaper printing.

Knob for adjusting the picture

SPREADING THE WORD
The phototelegraph, a technological advance in 1975, meant newspaper proofs could be sent quickly to every major city for simultaneous printing. It aided the centralized Soviet system as Party and government newspapers could appear at the same time in every city of the Soviet Union.

Viewing screen is just 1.18 in (3 cm) wide

On/off button

Volume control

COMMUNIST NEWS
The increase in literacy at the beginning of the 20th century led to the widespread availability of newspapers. *Pravda* began publication in a very small way in 1912 but reached a circulation of over 5 million during the Soviet era. Although its name means "truth," *Pravda* reported only what the Communist Party wanted the people to know, and facts were often ignored or distorted. The main mouthpiece of the Communist Party, the newspaper has survived in the new Russia but with a much reduced circulation.

EARLY TELEVISION
In 1931 the first Soviet television set was produced; it had only a tiny round screen. Transmissions began that year and by 1938 regular programs were being broadcast in Moscow and Leningrad. But only in the 1960s did television become available throughout the country. Like other areas of Soviet life, television was highly controlled and focused on the capital, with the same programs being relayed nationwide.

DOCUMENTING HISTORY
Sergei Eisenstein's films of the 1920s and 1930s are among the world's greatest. The scene above is from *October* (1927), about the Bolshevik Revolution. Under Stalin, filmmaking was rigidly controlled, but after his death exceptional films appeared again. These included Andrei Tarkovsky's *Rublev* (1966), about a famous icon painter, and Tengiz Abuladze's *Repentance* (1987), which deals with Stalinist terror.

Famous writers

RUSSIA'S FIRST-RECORDED literature was the 12th-century heroic poem, *The Song of Igor's Campaign*, about the capture of a Russian prince. But it was in the 19th century that Russian writing became world-famous. Pushkin and Mikhail Lermontov wrote fine romantic poetry and stories. Gogol's biting stories and the great novels of Tolstoy and Dostoevsky continued the Pushkin tradition. The last of the great 19th-century masters was Chekhov, who wrote brilliant plays and short stories. This great literary tradition continued in the 20th century with novels by Mikhail Bulgakov, Pasternak, and Solzhenitsyn, and the poetry of Anna Akhmatova and Osip Mandelstam, as well as new works by women writers, such as Lyudmila Petrushevskaya and Tatiana Tolstaya.

Quill pen with which Gogol wrote Dead Souls

Script of Gogol's story "A Terrible Vengeance," about a woman who falls under the spell of her father, a wizard

NIKOLAI GOGOL
Gogol (1809–52) was a dramatist, novelist, and short story writer. His works were a mixture of fantasy, horror, and humor. Gogol wrote about Cossacks and of life in the Ukraine. But his greatest works were *The Inspector General*, a play that made fun of provincial officials, and *Dead Souls*, a witty novel about serfs and landowners. Gogol burned his second volume of *Dead Souls* after a fanatical priest convinced him that the work was evil. Gogol died several days later – perhaps depriving the world of another masterpiece.

ALEXANDER PUSHKIN
Pushkin (1799–1837) is considered Russia's greatest poet. He was banished in 1824 for revolutionary and anti-religious writings. While barred from the capital, Pushkin was looked after by his nanny, about whom he wrote the poem "Companion in My Austere Days." Among his greatest works are the historical play *Boris Godunov*; a long poem, *The Bronze Horseman*, about a tragic flood in St. Petersburg; and many wonderful lyrical poems, which most Russians know by heart. Pushkin died, aged 37, fighting a duel, like the one in his greatest work, *Eugene Onegin*, against one of his beautiful wife's admirers.

Silver tea strainer given to Pushkin by his nanny

FYODOR DOSTOEVSKY
Dostoevsky (1821–81) is one of the world's greatest novelists but was often very poor. He was arrested in 1849 for belonging to a secret intellectual group, and sentenced to death. While standing before the firing squad, Dostoevsky was pardoned and sent to Siberia. His terrible experiences are reflected in his account of prison life, *The House of the Dead*. He also wrote *Crime and Punishment*, a novel about a murder.

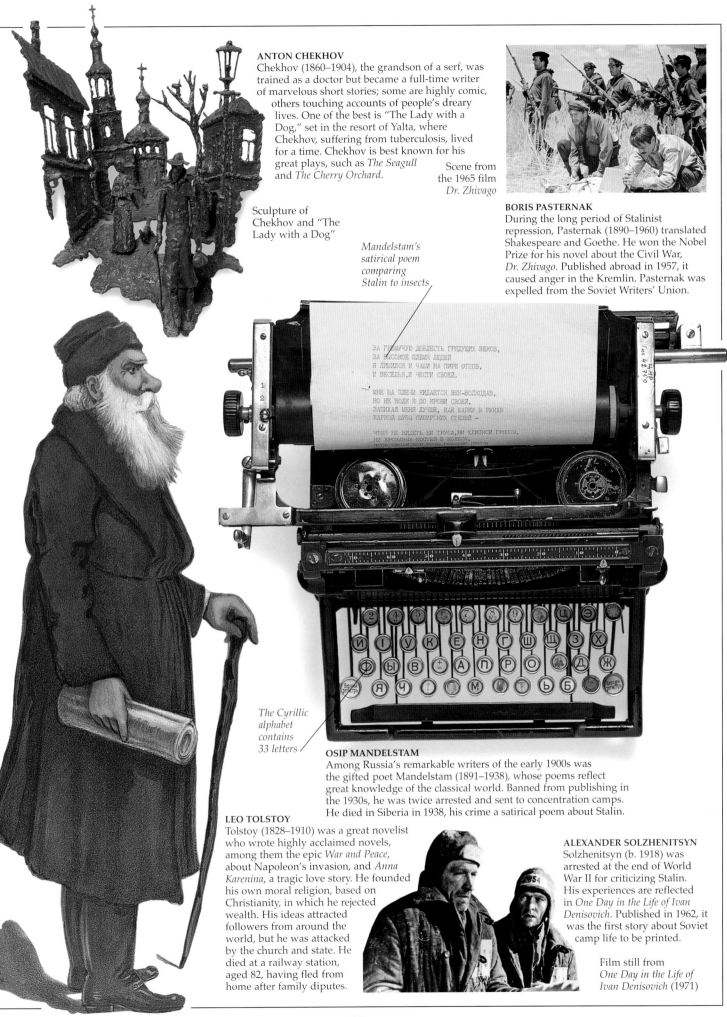

ANTON CHEKHOV

Chekhov (1860–1904), the grandson of a serf, was trained as a doctor but became a full-time writer of marvelous short stories; some are highly comic, others touching accounts of people's dreary lives. One of the best is "The Lady with a Dog," set in the resort of Yalta, where Chekhov, suffering from tuberculosis, lived for a time. Chekhov is best known for his great plays, such as *The Seagull* and *The Cherry Orchard*.

Scene from the 1965 film *Dr. Zhivago*

Sculpture of Chekhov and "The Lady with a Dog"

BORIS PASTERNAK

During the long period of Stalinist repression, Pasternak (1890–1960) translated Shakespeare and Goethe. He won the Nobel Prize for his novel about the Civil War, *Dr. Zhivago*. Published abroad in 1957, it caused anger in the Kremlin. Pasternak was expelled from the Soviet Writers' Union.

Mandelstam's satirical poem comparing Stalin to insects

The Cyrillic alphabet contains 33 letters

OSIP MANDELSTAM

Among Russia's remarkable writers of the early 1900s was the gifted poet Mandelstam (1891–1938), whose poems reflect great knowledge of the classical world. Banned from publishing in the 1930s, he was twice arrested and sent to concentration camps. He died in Siberia in 1938, his crime a satirical poem about Stalin.

LEO TOLSTOY

Tolstoy (1828–1910) was a great novelist who wrote highly acclaimed novels, among them the epic *War and Peace*, about Napoleon's invasion, and *Anna Karenina*, a tragic love story. He founded his own moral religion, based on Christianity, in which he rejected wealth. His ideas attracted followers from around the world, but he was attacked by the church and state. He died at a railway station, aged 82, having fled from home after family diputes.

ALEXANDER SOLZHENITSYN

Solzhenitsyn (b. 1918) was arrested at the end of World War II for criticizing Stalin. His experiences are reflected in *One Day in the Life of Ivan Denisovich*. Published in 1962, it was the first story about Soviet camp life to be printed.

Film still from *One Day in the Life of Ivan Denisovich* (1971)

Art and icons

In ARCHITECTURE, PAINTING, and sculpture Russians throughout the ages have shown special feeling for color and shape. Religious art (icons, frescoes, and mosaics) dominated until the 17th century, when other subjects – portraits and landscapes – became popular. In the 19th century the Wanderers (a society of artists who portrayed the realities of life), led by Ilya Repin, painted ordinary people and scenes from Russian history. In the early 1900s, Mikhail Vrubel's unique style of painting influenced modern artists like Malevich, Kandinsky, and Chagall. At first vivid and daring, Soviet art was soon forced to portray positive images of Soviet life. Modern abstract art was forced underground but is free in the new Russia.

DISCOVERY OF BLACK GEORGE

Icons of St. George and the dragon were popular, but usually the horse was white, not black. This rare 14th-century icon was discovered in 1959 in a northern village near Arkhangelsk. It was being used as a shutter for a barn and was hidden by a thick layer of paint. The icon was spied as the shutter was being stripped for repainting. Moscow restorers carefully cleaned the shutter to reveal this delightful, well-preserved icon.

Pestle for grinding pigments to a fine powder

NATURAL PIGMENTS

Pigments (colors) used in icon painting are derived from the natural world. White comes from lead, black from ash. From clay comes ocher. Bright red is from vermilion, a mercury compound; gold occurs naturally.

HISTORY OF ICON PAINTING

In Byzantium, icons painted by formal rules were usually solemn and severe. But in Russia icon painting gradually took on a gentler, more emotional character. Andrei Rublev (c. 1360–1430) was one of the greatest Russian icon painters. He composed this beautiful picture, *The Old Testament Trinity*, of God the Father, Son, and Holy Ghost, in disguise, as guests of Abraham.

Bright blue lapis lazuli comes from silica rock

Red ocher

Gold

Vermilion (cinnabar)

Ground lapis lazuli

Icon restoration

Restoration of ancient icons is a painstakingly slow process. In the past, darkened icons were repainted – the new image on top of the old. In Soviet times restorers devised methods of preserving each layer.

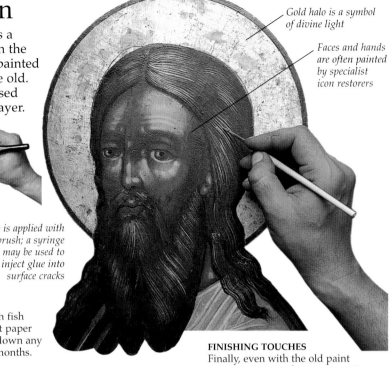

Gold halo is a symbol of divine light

Faces and hands are often painted by specialist icon restorers

Icons are blackened over time by candle smoke

Glue is applied with a brush; a syringe may be used to inject glue into surface cracks

Rublev's figures, bowed in thought, are painted in soft, luminous colors

STRENGTHENING
Icon is strengthened by soaking with fish glue until supple. Glued transparent paper is then ironed onto surface to stick down any peeling paint and left for up to six months.

Film is weighted down over ether to prevent evaporation

Ether is dabbed on to icon through material

CLEANING THE SURFACE
Glued paper is removed by wetting. After careful testing, the icon is cleaned with ether. It can take an hour or more to scrape away dirt from a small segment. Care is taken not to overlap a previously cleaned section. Oil and turpentine complete the cleaning.

Lighter sections have already been cleaned

Dirt is removed carefully with a sharp knife

FINISHING TOUCHES
Finally, even with the old paint secure and clean, there are usually fragments where the image has entirely disappeared. To repaint these sections, some Russian icon restorers use watercolors and not the egg tempera paint of the original artists. They want future restorers to know from the type of paint where the icon has been restored, and where the original painting has survived.

BEGINNINGS OF REALISM
Ilya Repin (1844–1930) came from a peasant family; he painted not only portraits but also controversial political and historical scenes. His *Religious Procession in Kursk* shows the poverty and blind faith of the people, and the hostility of the mounted police.

SOVIET ART
By the 1930s artists had to obey the Communist Party policy that all art should reflect a positive view of Soviet life. Stalin and other Soviet leaders were portrayed as wise and kind by artists like Alexander Gerasimov (1881–1963). His namesake, Sergei Gerasimov (1885–1964), in his *Collective Farm Festivities* presents a false view of jolly life on the farm. It was painted in 1937, the worst year of the Great Terror, when hundreds of thousands, including farmers, were arrested.

Malevich used these shapes in textile and pottery designs during the 1920s

ABSTRACT ART
The burst of creativity in Russia in all the arts at the beginning of the 20th century was reflected in the appearance of a modern abstract art. The uneducated but immensely talented Kasimir Malevich (1878–1935) experimented with color and geometric shapes to suggest force, motion, and space.

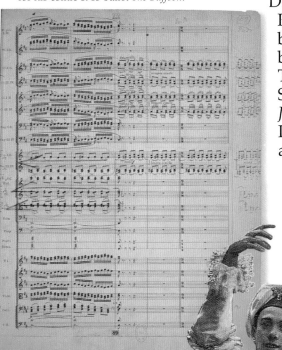

THE BUFFOON
A most original and witty composer of the 20th century, Sergei Prokofiev (1891–1953) wrote vivid and exciting music for the ballet *Romeo and Juliet*. This brilliant scenery was for his comic 1915 ballet *The Buffoon*.

Music and dance

THE ORIGINS OF ST. PETERSBURG'S Kirov Ballet go back to the 18th century. In 1776, the Moscow Bolshoi ballet began, using orphan children as dancers. At the end of the 19th century, ballet choreographer Marius Petipa created *Sleeping Beauty* and *Swan Lake*, ballets written to music by Tchaikovsky, the first of many great Russian composers, including Stravinsky and Prokofiev, to write for the ballet. From 1909 on, Sergei Diaghilev, founder of the Ballets Russes, sponsored radical ballets that burst like bombshells onto the world. The best new ballets of the Soviet era include *Romeo and Juliet*, *Spartacus*, and *The Golden Age*. Pavlova, Nijinsky, Ulanova, and Nureyev are some of Russia's greatest dancers.

A SHOCKING COMPOSER
An original composer, Igor Stravinsky (1882–1971) shocked the public with his modern rhythms. He composed ballets for Diaghilev, such as the popular *Petrushka* (score sheet above). Stravinsky left Russia during World War I, but his work continued to be inspired by Russian folk music.

DIAGHILEV'S GENIUS
Sergei Diaghilev (1872–1929), manager of the Ballets Russes, attracted talented composers, choreographers, and artists, who together created outstanding ballets. He employed Mikhail Fokine as choreographer (creator of dance) to devise most of the company's famous ballets, including *Narcissus*. This brilliant costume for *Narcissus* was designed by Russian artist Léon Bakst, who excelled in the use of extravagant style and color.

"GOD OF DANCE"
After studying ballet, Vaslav Nijinsky (1889–1950) became a leading dancer of the Maryinsky Theater in St. Petersburg. Joining Diaghilev's Ballets Russes, he not only danced such roles as *Petrushka* but also choreographed daring ballets like *The Rite of Spring* and *The Afternoon of a Faun*. But Nijinsky's relationship with Diaghilev deteriorated and by 1917 he had grown paranoid and withdrawn. From 1918 on he spent his life in a mental hospital. His career had lasted just 10 years.

Nijinsky as Armida's page in *Le Pavillon d'Armide*

PRIMA BALLERINA
Anna Pavlova (1882–1931) was prima ballerina at St. Petersburg's Maryinsky Theater for several years before joining the Ballets Russes in 1909 and starring in Fokine's *Les Sylphides*. She finally left Russia during World War I and settled in London, where she formed her own small company. Pavlova was a superb classical ballerina with wonderful technique. She is shown here dancing in Tchaikovsky's *Swan Lake*.

Pavlova dancing the Dying Swan

REVOLUTIONARY BALLET
The *Rite of Spring* had music by Stravinsky, choreography by Nijinsky, and lyrics and costumes by the artist Nikolai Roerich. The wild drumming music was considered so outrageous at its first performance in Paris in 1913 that a near-riot broke out. The Paris performance, however, was followed by a successful London debut in the same year. *The Rite of Spring* is now considered a landmark in 20th-century ballet.

Cap by Roerich for a young man in The Rite of Spring

PAGAN RUSSIA
The subject of *The Rite of Spring* was pagan Russia before it became Christian. The ballet is divided into two parts: the first celebrates the adoration of the earth, while in the second, a chosen maiden dances herself to death as a sacrifice to the earth.

Squares, circles, waves, and dots are the basis of the design for the maiden's costume in The Rite of Spring

FOLK MUSIC
Russian folk music grew out of the pagan Slavs' ritual songs used in festivals and ceremonies. In medieval times people sang epic ballads, playing a one-string instrument, the *gusli*. Jesters entertained with comical songs and satires. Here, a 19th-century accordionist plays as peasants dance.

The balalaika normally has three strings and a fretted fingerboard

MUSICAL INSTRUMENTS
In early Russia the *domra*, a 3- or 4-stringed instrument with a rounded soundboard, and the *balalaika* with 3 strings and a triangular soundboard were popular. Among wind instruments the *rozhok* (shepherd's horn) and *dudka* (pipe) were played. The *balalaika* is still widely played, especially in villages and folk music bands.

The triangular soundboard is often painted with mythical figures

Crafts and traditions

In the past the isolation of Russian villages and the long, snowbound winters allowed peasants much free time to engage in craftwork. The abundance of wood encouraged carving; delightful wooden toys and domestic utensils, including the traditional drinking dippers (*kovsh*), were made in nearly every village. Some, like the colorful distaffs (*prialki*) for spinning, were brightly painted. Intricate embroidery and handmade lace are still produced in the northern towns. Icon painters, forbidden by the Bolsheviks in 1922 to pursue their craft, began to make lacquer boxes decorated with illustrations of fairy tales. Metal and pottery ware and clay figurines also have a long tradition.

SPINNING FLAX
Until recently, spinning and weaving took place in nearly every peasant home, and distaffs (*prialk*i) were part of the essential household equipment. The women above, sitting on the porch of a large wooden house in northern Russia, are spinning flax using traditional distaffs.

COLORFUL EMBROIDERY
In medieval times, when Russian women were confined to the home, they occupied themselves by establishing workshops. Here they not only fashioned their family's clothes but also embroidered elaborate cloths and robes for church purposes. Humbler people decorated their linen towels, wall hangings, and dresses with embroidery or drawn-thread designs of ancient origin. The 19th-century linen towel (above) embroidered with red thread (*kumach*), comes from the Vologda region, north of Moscow.

WOODEN SPINNER
The distaff, made of pine or birch, is a long board with a base on which the spinner sits. The wool or flax is held by the round projections at the upper end and pulled by the spinner to make a thread. Distaffs are usually gaily painted with designs of flowers or animals – or, as here, the lion and the unicorn. It was common for a husband to present a distaff to his new bride.

Brightly painted distaff is carved out of pine

Seat for spinner, who holds the board in place with her weight

DIPPING DUCK
In medieval Russia, the handled dipper, *kovsh*, was commonly used as a bowl for holding drinks. Dippers made from precious metals were often presented to important people by the tsars. The ancient form of the dipper is based on the shape of a duck or the prow of a boat.

This painted wood dipper, carved with a duck's head and tail, was made in the early 19th century

Wooden dippers are mostly made from pine, but sometimes birch is used

Duck's head makes a useful handle to hold the bowllike dipper

Brocade embroidered with gold thread

GINGERBREAD TREAT
In Russian villages, crisp gingerbread was customarily baked in carved wooden molds to celebrate weddings, funerals, and church holidays, and is still considered a great treat. The molds have a long history, but by 1800 traditional designs of animals, birds, and the flowering bush – a sign of rebirth – began to change as new patterns from news sheets, *(lubok, p. 42)*, with their cartoonlike illustrations, became more widespread. This mold, made in the early part of the 19th century, depicts a bearded peasant dressed up for a festive occasion.

Mother-of-pearl geese and flowers decorate the headdress

Ribbons were tied in a large bow at the back of the head

The water carrier is a favorite subject among clay modelers

The rooster is a popular figure in all types of Russian folk art

FESTIVE HEADDRESS
This beautiful bonnet, or *kokoshnik*, comes from northern European Russia, near Arkhangelsk. Made at the end of the 18th century, it is open at the back, which means it is for an unmarried girl: married women had to cover all their hair. Glass stones and mother-of-pearl are sewn on to a brocade background, which is stiffened with canvas. The headdress would have been worn for weddings and other important festivals, and was handed down from mother to daughter.

CLAY FIGURINES
Homemade clay figurines were once part of a pre-Christian magic ritual, but by the 19th century were used as toys. They are still made at Dymkovo, now part of the city of Kirov, on the Vyatka River. The toys are shaped from potter's clay mixed with river sand. They are then fired, whitened with chalk, and painted in strong colors. The craft, which was dying at the end of the 19th century, was revived during the Soviet period.

Bread and salt are offered on an embroidered towel

Salt is placed in a pot or in a dent on the top of the loaf

Pink silk ribbons stream out at the back

BREAD-AND-SALT GREETING
Russians traditionally greet important guests by offering bread and salt on an embroidered towel held by the hosts' youngest daughter. The guest breaks off a piece of bread, dips it in salt, and eats it. Salt was considered such a luxury in old Russia that it was stored in a strong warehouse in Moscow on the Solyanka, or Salt Street. Russians are very hospitable to this day, and welcome and offer food to guests, however unexpected.

Childhood

CHILDREN ARE WELL LOOKED AFTER in Russian society. Day care is provided for children whose parents work outside the home. Children start school at age 6 and finish by the age of 14 (16 if they continue their secondary education). Some schools still use Soviet school uniforms, which resemble those of tsarist times: girls wear brown dresses with white pinafores, boys wear blue tunics and trousers. Soviet children belonged to organizations that emphasized Communist ideals. Russia's children's literature and theater are among the best in the world.

BABY SWADDLING
It is customary in Russia to wrap babies up tightly in swaddling clothes for the first few months of life. Some people believe that this helps to straighten a baby's bones. Left swaddled for long periods of time, the babies are only occasionally unwrapped for a bath and a romp. Outside the hospitals, swaddling is gradually becoming less fashionable.

DRESSED LIKE MOTHER
This outfit from Orel province, southwest of Moscow, was typical of everyday wear for a little peasant girl in 19th-century Russia. It imitates her mother's clothes in that it consists of a jumper, or *sarafan*, with a long-sleeved blouse underneath. The printed cotton would have been bought in a store, but the outfit was sewn at home.

Strips of lace and other material decorate the dress

Felt boots are surprisingly waterproof on the ice

OUTDOOR GEAR
Children need to dress warmly in the cold Russian winter. This little boy, gliding down an ice slide, wears a warm coat, scarf, mittens, a fur-lined *shapka* cap with flaps to cover the forehead and ears, and felt boots, *valenki*, that are very warm in the snow.

WOODEN TOYS
Until the 20th century, Russian toys were made at home out of wood, the cheapest and most readily available material. Wood was made into puppets and all sorts of animals, from cows to bears. Colorful *matryoshka* nesting dolls were a favorite toy; now they are popular tourist souvenirs.

Matryoshka peasant dolls fit inside one another – the biggest one in the set holds the rest

These dolls are meant to be a family, with the baby as the smallest

SUMMER CAMPS

During their three-month summer vacation, many Russian children enjoy the green countryside at a summer camp or country home (*dacha*). This is an important respite from the cities' crowded and noisy apartment complexes. Summer camps are organized through schools, or parents' employers, and are often held in the country houses of the former nobles.

COMMUNIST YOUTH GROUPS

Nearly all Soviet children between the ages of 7 and 10 belonged to the Octobrists; those ages 10 to 14 belonged to the Young Pioneers, while young people aged 14 to 28 joined the Komsomol (Young Communist League). These groups, which taught loyalty to the Communist Party, also provided hobby clubs the way Girl and Boy Scouts do. In the 1930s, however, Soviet brainwashing of children was so intense that some even betrayed their parents to the authorities. After 14-year-old Pavlik Morozov informed on his parents for helping kulaks (rich peasants), his father was shot. Pavlik was then murdered by his angry uncle, but became a Soviet hero.

The bear is a favorite character in Russian fairy tales

Girl Pioneers wore a blouse and skirt and, like the boys, red scarves

CHILDREN'S LITERATURE

Russia is rich in children's literature. Traditional fairy tales (*skazky*) were collected and vividly illustrated in the early 20th century. A famous character is the terrifying witch Baba Yaga, who has iron teeth and lives in a hut that stands on chicken's legs. Two recent children writers are Samuel Marshak, who wrote fairy tales, and Kornei Chukovsky, who wrote a Russian version of *Dr. Dolittle* called *Dr. Aibolit* ("Dr. Ouchithurts.")

SCHOOLS FOR THE GIFTED

The Soviets established special schools in the cities to encourage those talented in mathematics, languages, music, and sports. This little girl is studying dance in a ballet school. Only a few children get into the school; they have to show great talent. Along with learning ballet, they take the usual school courses.

National pastimes

IN SUMMER RUSSIANS enjoy swimming, long walks in the countryside, and fishing. Winter activities include skating, cross-country skiing, and ice fishing. In autumn people of all ages love to go mushroom picking in the woods. Popular sports include soccer and ice hockey, at which Russia is a world leader. Tennis is rapidly becoming popular. Russians are also fond of gymnastics and perform well at many sports in the Olympics. Favorite games include chess and dominoes; older people can often be seen playing these in city parks. Even though most people have modern bathrooms, the weekly steam bath is still a regular custom in both the city and the countryside.

CHESS CHAMPIONS
The game of chess came to Russia from China 1,000 years ago. After the 1917 Revolution, chess was strongly encouraged, and clubs were organized in schools and factories. Many recent world champions have been Russian.

Buckets of this sort are used in steam baths for washing, or to throw water on the stove to create more steam

MUSHROOM PICKING
In the damp late summer and early autumn, thick clusters of mushrooms spring up in the woods and fields. Armed with baskets and buckets, people scour the countryside, and even city parks, for the many varieties of edible mushrooms. They take their trophies home to eat right away, or to dry for future use.

Birch twig bunches for beating dirt out of one's pores are sold at the entrances to steam baths

STEAM BATHS
Russians delight in their weekly steam bath (*banya*). Many villages have their own steam baths, while in the cities baths are found in every district. Friday and Saturday nights are the busiest, the traditional times for a good scrub. People steam their bodies to extreme temperatures, lash themselves with birch twigs (*venik*), then plunge into a cold bath or, if in the countryside in winter, roll in the snow.

Mushrooms are strung together, hung up, and dried in a warm kitchen; they last a long time

COUNTRY REFUGE
In summer it is customary for city people to stay at a *dacha*, or country retreat. Children swim and play at the *dacha*, while adults fish, swim, tend the garden, walk in the woods, and enjoy a life in complete contrast to the bustle of the busy city.

SLIPPERY SLOPES
In the deep cold of winter, ice slides can be made quickly on any slope, gentle or steep. Water poured down the slopes freezes rapidly. Children all over Russia enjoy such slides; some use sleds, but many just slither down in their thickly padded clothes (p. 52). Elaborate wooden slides like this one were built in places with few hills, such as St. Petersburg.

Chess is a popular game among children, who are usually encouraged to learn while still at school

Teapot rests conveniently on top for a quick refill of hot water when needed

TEA DRINKING
Russians love to drink weak black tea all day long. To have the tea readily available, they use a samovar ("self-boiling") urn. The water in this traditional samovar is heated by a central tube that is filled with pine cones and kindled by charcoal. The tea in the pot on top of the samovar can then be continually refreshed with the boiling water. Nowadays, samovars are usually heated by electricity.

Top opens here and pine cones are placed in the central tube

These wooden shutters keep out draughts during the long, harsh winters

A dacha *can be anything from a small wooden cottage to a sizable villa. Even a single room in a humble country cottage can be a* dacha

Screws attached these 1820s ice skates to warm boots

Ornate air vents provide an inlet for the oxygen needed to keep the pine cones alight

Fine samovars, such as this silver one, were made in the metal workshops of Tula, south of Moscow

Hot water to fill the teapot is obtained by turning the tap

ON FROZEN PONDS
Outdoor ice-skating has long been a national pastime in Russia for people of all ages. In winter, frozen ponds or flooded artificial rinks attract crowds of skaters who glide gracefully to piped music. The ice is regularly swept free of snow, and heated cabins allow skaters to put on their skates in comfort. These elegant skates belonged to Pavel Nakhimov, a famous Russian admiral, who in 1853 defeated the Turkish fleet during the Crimean War.

Annual festivals

THE IMPORTANT FESTIVALS of the year in Russia begin with New Year's, which is celebrated like the Western Christmas. Grandfather Frost and the Snow Maiden distribute presents, and on New Year's Eve families gather around a decorated fir tree for dinner and gift opening. Christmas is celebrated on January 7, because the Russian Orthodox Church follows the Julian calendar, which is 13 days behind the Gregorian calendar used elsewhere. Easter, the main religious festival of the year, remained popular, even in Soviet times. Military parades on May Day and the anniversary of the Revolution are no longer celebrated.

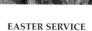

EASTER SERVICE
The service begins late on the eve of Easter and continues all night. At midnight the congregation, carrying lit candles, follows the priest around the outside of the church; this commemorates the women who came to the tomb of Christ and found it empty. At the doors of the church the priest proclaims, "Christ is risen." The worshipers joyfully reply, "He is risen indeed," and kiss their neighbors.

BREAKING THE FAST
As dawn breaks, the Easter service finishes, and the worshipers disperse to their homes to break their long fast with special Easter foods and colored eggs. The Easter cake (*kulich*), and the *paskha* (a sweet made of curd cheese) contain ingredients forbidden during Lent. Guests, who stop by all day, are offered the cakes.

Golden-domed monastery

On the side of the paskha *is a cross, or "XB," which stands for "Christ has risen"*

Men dress up in red robes and pass out pancakes to the crowds

PAINTED EGGS
In the week before Easter, everyone is busy painting eggs. Some are just boiled with onion skins, making lovely mottled brown and yellow colors. Others, with the yolk and white blown out through small pinholes in the end, are painted elaborately with religious or festive scenes. The eggs are eaten at the feast after the long Easter service.

This amusing painting shows a brown bear, one of Russia's national symbols, enjoying a sleigh ride

CELEBRATION OF LENT
The eve of Lent is traditionally the time of the butter festival, *maslenitsa*, when pancakes are eaten in large amounts. With snow still thick on the ground, some hardy people celebrate by breaking holes in frozen lakes and rivers and diving into the icy water.

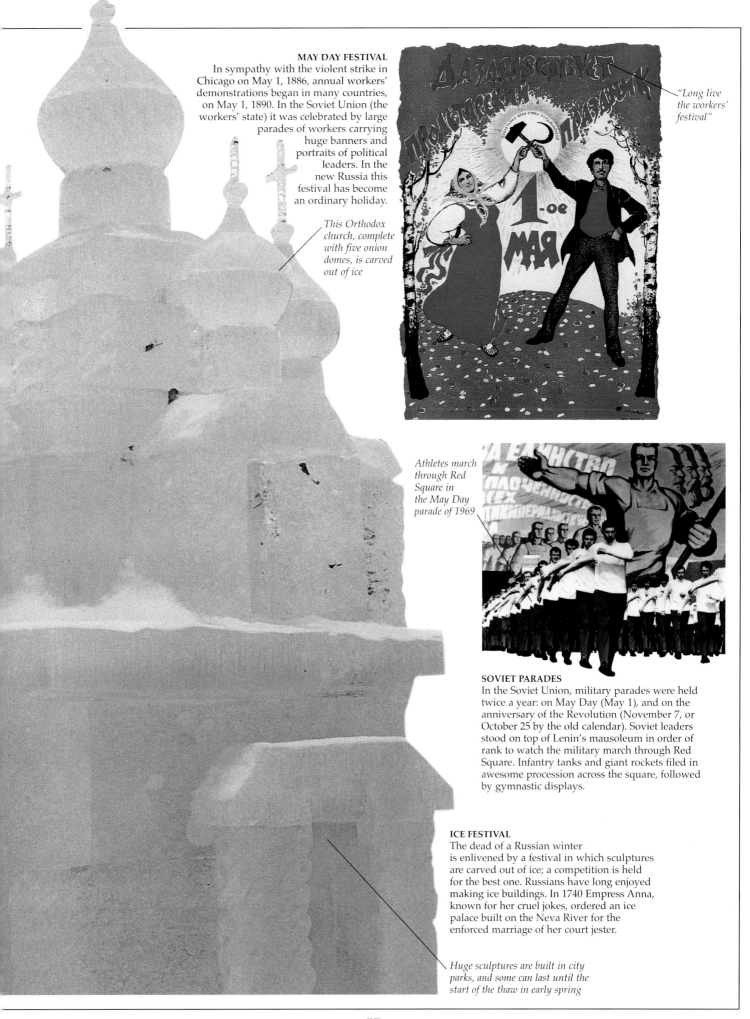

MAY DAY FESTIVAL

In sympathy with the violent strike in Chicago on May 1, 1886, annual workers' demonstrations began in many countries, on May 1, 1890. In the Soviet Union (the workers' state) it was celebrated by large parades of workers carrying huge banners and portraits of political leaders. In the new Russia this festival has become an ordinary holiday.

This Orthodox church, complete with five onion domes, is carved out of ice

"Long live the workers' festival"

Athletes march through Red Square in the May Day parade of 1969

SOVIET PARADES

In the Soviet Union, military parades were held twice a year: on May Day (May 1), and on the anniversary of the Revolution (November 7, or October 25 by the old calendar). Soviet leaders stood on top of Lenin's mausoleum in order of rank to watch the military march through Red Square. Infantry tanks and giant rockets filed in awesome procession across the square, followed by gymnastic displays.

ICE FESTIVAL

The dead of a Russian winter is enlivened by a festival in which sculptures are carved out of ice; a competition is held for the best one. Russians have long enjoyed making ice buildings. In 1740 Empress Anna, known for her cruel jokes, ordered an ice palace built on the Neva River for the enforced marriage of her court jester.

Huge sculptures are built in city parks, and some can last until the start of the thaw in early spring

The new Russia

IN AUGUST 1991 HARDLINE Communists staged a coup (overthrow)
against President Gorbachev and his reforms. The newly elected
president of the Russian Republic, Boris Yeltsin, occupied the White
House (Parliament building), in Moscow, and opposed the coup. Moscow
citizens rallied behind Yeltsin and within three days the coup collapsed.
At the end of 1991, the Soviet Union fell apart and the Russian
Federation, led by Yeltsin, was born. In October 1993, Yeltsin dissolved
the hardline parliament, which fiercely opposed his reforms. Again the
parliament was occupied, this time by Communists and nationalists.
Yeltsin used force; about 150 people died, but the hardliners were
defeated. Since then, Russia has kept moving toward a market economy.
Despite crime and corruption, life is improving for many people.

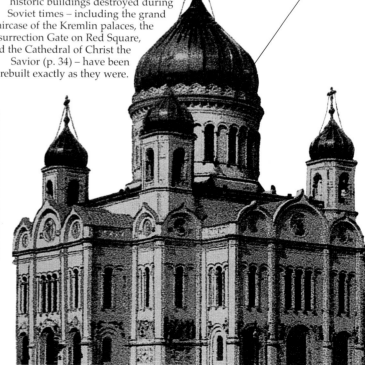

*The Communist
hammer and sickle
flag came down
on Christmas
Day, 1991*

NEW ECONOMY
In 1992 Russia attempted
to change abruptly from a
state-owned economy to a
free-market system. At
first there was confusion
and huge price rises as the
ruble (Russian currency)
crashed in value. The
economic reforms were
then slowed down, and
gradually the value of the
ruble, which had never
before operated in a free
market, settled to about
5,000 to the U.S. dollar.

*Cathedral of Christ
the Savior was
rebuilt in 1997 on
its original site,
where a swimming
pool had stood
since 1958*

*In 1912, a workman or
shopkeeper would earn
500 rubles a year*

*In the 1990s,
500 rubles can
only buy one egg*

RESTORING THE PAST
Russian cities are taking on a
fresh look as new businesses start and
buildings are restored. Some important
historic buildings destroyed during
Soviet times – including the grand
staircase of the Kremlin palaces, the
Resurrection Gate on Red Square,
and the Cathedral of Christ the
Savior (p. 34) – have been
rebuilt exactly as they were.

LAST LEADER OF THE SOVIET UNION
In 1985 Mikhail Gorbachev, the new Soviet leader, introduced
a policy of openness (*glasnost*) followed by cautious reforms
(*perestroika*). But he came under attack both by Communists
opposing reform and radicals who wanted more democracy.
After the failed coup of August 1991, Gorbachev was freed
but found Yeltsin now in control and resigned four months
later. But his reforms had made possible the new Russia.

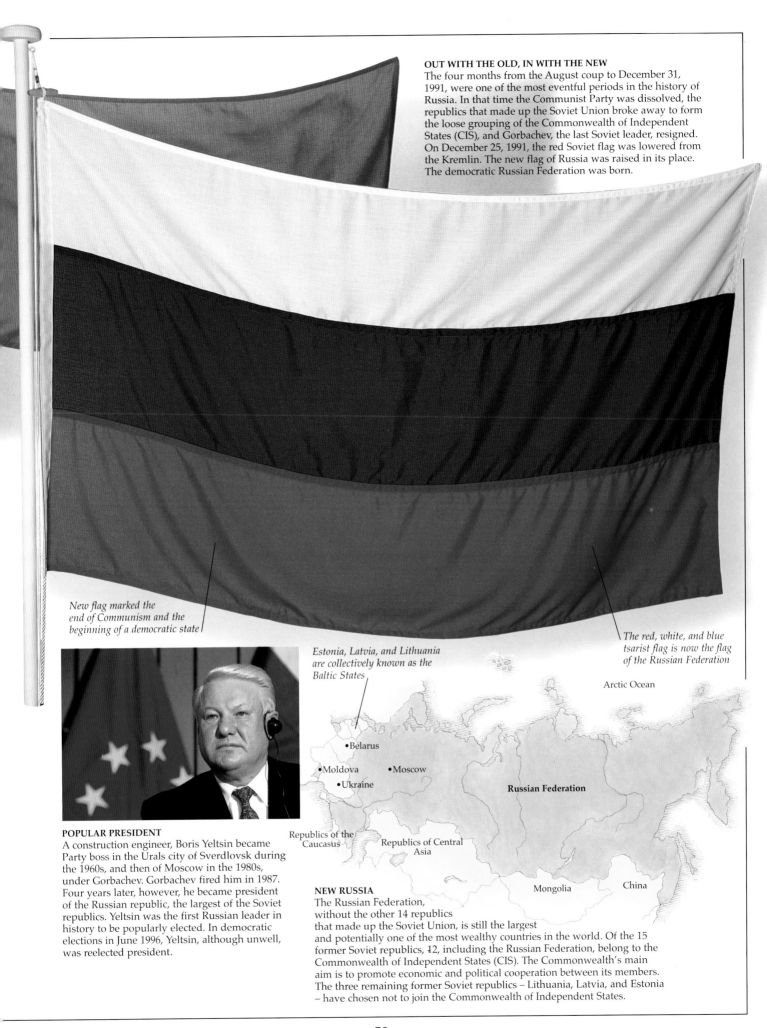

OUT WITH THE OLD, IN WITH THE NEW

The four months from the August coup to December 31, 1991, were one of the most eventful periods in the history of Russia. In that time the Communist Party was dissolved, the republics that made up the Soviet Union broke away to form the loose grouping of the Commonwealth of Independent States (CIS), and Gorbachev, the last Soviet leader, resigned. On December 25, 1991, the red Soviet flag was lowered from the Kremlin. The new flag of Russia was raised in its place. The democratic Russian Federation was born.

New flag marked the end of Communism and the beginning of a democratic state

Estonia, Latvia, and Lithuania are collectively known as the Baltic States

The red, white, and blue tsarist flag is now the flag of the Russian Federation

Arctic Ocean

- Belarus
- Moldova
- Moscow
- Ukraine

Russian Federation

Republics of the Caucasus

Republics of Central Asia

Mongolia   China

POPULAR PRESIDENT

A construction engineer, Boris Yeltsin became Party boss in the Urals city of Sverdlovsk during the 1960s, and then of Moscow in the 1980s, under Gorbachev. Gorbachev fired him in 1987. Four years later, however, he became president of the Russian republic, the largest of the Soviet republics. Yeltsin was the first Russian leader in history to be popularly elected. In democratic elections in June 1996, Yeltsin, although unwell, was reelected president.

NEW RUSSIA

The Russian Federation, without the other 14 republics that made up the Soviet Union, is still the largest and potentially one of the most wealthy countries in the world. Of the 15 former Soviet republics, 12, including the Russian Federation, belong to the Commonwealth of Independent States (CIS). The Commonwealth's main aim is to promote economic and political cooperation between its members. The three remaining former Soviet republics – Lithuania, Latvia, and Estonia – have chosen not to join the Commonwealth of Independent States.

Index

Acknowledgments

Dorling Kindersley would like to thank:
Tamara Igumnova, Lyudmila Savchenko, Svetlana Zhizhina, Irina Poltusova, Tatiana Sizova, Yelena Smirnova, Yulia Gudovich, Lyudmila Dementieva, and Luiza Yefimova at the History Museum, Moscow; Pavel Rubinin of the Kapitza Museum, Moscow; Professor Roman Shatalov and Tatiana Susorova at the Polytechnic Museum, Moscow; Alexander Nikonov at the Museum of Armed Forces, Moscow; Tamara Shumnaya and Irina Orlova at the Museum of the Revolution, Moscow; Alexander Chepurnoi; Sergei Romaniuk; Yevgenia Grishina; Kate Cook; Zoya Yevgenyevna of Red Square Publications; Ella Piatigorsky; Joyce Roberson and Steven Platt of the Russian Orthodox Church; David Buckton at the British Museum; Cornelissen & Son, London; Paul Cornish, Andy Hutcheson, and David Fearon at the Imperial War Museum; The Britain-Russia Centre, London; The Earl of Pembroke and Trustees of the Wilton House Trust; and photographers Ian Jackson and Andy Brown.

Consultant: Geoffrey Murrell

Researcher: Robert Graham

Illustrator: John Woodcock

Modelmaker: Peter Griffiths

Index: Marion Dent

Jacket: Chris Branfield

Design and editorial assistance: Susila Baybars, Goldberry Broad, Maggie Tingle, Darren Troughton, and Jake Williamson

Picture credits
The publisher would like to thank the following for their kind permission to reproduce the photographs:

(a = above, c = center, b = below, l = left, r = right, t = top)

AISA, Barcelona: 22t, 23cb, 44c, 44b, 48bl.
Bridgeman Art Library, London/New York: The Fine Art Society, London 48 cr; Hermitage, St. Petersburg: Portrait Peter I (1723) Grigory Semyonovich 20bla; Portrait Catherine I (1729–96) Feodor Rokotov 20b; Kremlin Museums, Moscow 20cla; Lords Gallery, London 39c; Bibliotheque de L'Opera, Paris 48tl; Musée d'Orsay, Paris: Coronation of Nicholas II (1852–1929) Henri Gervex 24cl; Petit Palais, Geneva: Russian Peasants (1869–1940) Andreevich Malyavin 49cr; Private Collection 34-35b; State Russian Museum, St. Petersburg: Portrait of Rastrelli (1700–71) Pietro Rotari 28tr; Stapleton Collection 28ca; Tretyakov Gallery, Moscow: Tsar Ivan IV (1530–84) Vitor Mikhailovich 20cr; Religious Procession (1880–83) Ilya Efimovich Repin 47cbr.
E.T. Archive: 20c, 48cl.
Mary Evans Picture Library: 9tr, 12bl, 16t, 17tl, 17bl, 19tl, 21br, 33br, 39tl, 45l, 48br.
Hulton Getty: 8tl, 8b, 37t, 57.
Giraudon: 23c; Lauros 19tr, 21cra.
The Ronald Grant Archive: 43br, 45tr, 45b.
Robert Harding: Paul van Riel 39cb.
Natural History Picture Agency: Mirko Stelzner 11trb.
Michael Holford: 14br.
The Hutchison Library: 52cl, 55t; © Andzey 56t, 56br.
The Interior Archive: 29tl.
Michael Jenner: 28cl, 29cl, 36r, 37l.
David King Collection: 14cl,15cbr,16cl, 20tl, 21tr, 30cl, 30bl, 30br, 31tl, 32cl, 33tl, 34cl, 34cl, 35tl, 35cl, 35bl, 36t, 38tl, 38c, 42b, 43tl, 43tr, 46t, 47bl, 52tl, 53tl, 57tr, 58br.
Frank Lane Picture Agency: 10tr.
Mander & Mitchenson: 49tr.
John Massey Stewart: 28c, 29c.
Novosti Photo Library: 15tr, 18cl, 23cl, 26-27cb, 30cb, 30-31b, 40cla, 40clb, 41cr, 41b, 47br, 50c, 53c.
Planet Earth Pictures: William P. Paton 11b.
Nikolai Rakhmanonov: 14t, 18tl, 21c, 24tl, 25tr, 25c.
Rex Features: Sipa Press 58bl, 58b.
Ellen Rooney: 18bl, 28-29b, 29tl, 29ca.
Oxford Scientific Films: Martyn Colbeck 11cr; Mark Hamblin 11bra; Zig Leszczynski 10cl; Owen Newman 11trb.
Topham Picturepoint: 24b.
Trip: M. Jenkin 27tr; B. Turner 26-27ca; N. & J. Wiseman 37br.
Victoria & Albert Museum: 49tl, 49l.

Jacket: all DK special photography, with the exception of:
The Bridgeman Art Library: back tr; **Giraudon:** front c; **Novosti Photo Library:** back bl; **Ellen Rooney:** front r; **Trip:** back br.

SUBJECTS

HISTORY
AFRICA
ANCIENT CHINA
ARMS & ARMOR
BATTLE
CASTLE
COWBOY
EXPLORER
KNIGHT
MEDIEVAL LIFE
MYTHOLOGY
NORTH AMERICAN INDIAN
PIRATE
PRESIDENTS
RUSSIA
SHIPWRECK
TITANIC
VIKING
WITCHES & MAGIC-MAKERS

ANCIENT WORLDS
ANCIENT EGYPT
ANCIENT GREECE
ANCIENT ROME
AZTEC, INCA & MAYA
BIBLE LANDS
MUMMY
PYRAMID

THE BEGINNINGS OF LIFE
ARCHEOLOGY
DINOSAUR
EARLY HUMANS
PREHISTORIC LIFE

THE ARTS
BOOK
COSTUME
DANCE
FILM
MUSIC

TECHNOLOGY
BOAT
CAR
FLYING MACHINE
FUTURE
INVENTION
SPACE EXPLORATION
TRAIN

PAINTING
GOYA
IMPRESSIONISM
LEONARDO & HIS TIMES
MANET
MONET
PERSPECTIVE
RENAISSANCE
VAN GOGH
WATERCOLOR

SCIENCE

ASTRONOMY

CHEMISTRY

EARTH

ECOLOGY

ELECTRICITY

ELECTRONICS

ENERGY

EVOLUTION

FORCE & MOTION

HUMAN BODY

LIFE

LIGHT

MATTER

MEDICINE

SKELETON

TECHNOLOGY

TIME & SPACE

SPORT

BASEBALL

FOOTBALL

OLYMPICS

SOCCER

SPORTS

ANIMALS

AMPHIBIAN

BIRD

BUTTERFLY & MOTH

CAT

DOG

EAGLE &
BIRDS OF PREY

ELEPHANT

FISH

GORILLA,
MONKEY & APE

HORSE

INSECT

MAMMAL

REPTILE

SHARK

WHALE

HABITATS

ARCTIC & ANTARCTIC

DESERT

JUNGLE

OCEAN

POND & RIVER

SEASHORE

THE EARTH

CRYSTAL & GEM

FOSSIL

HURRICANE &
TORNADO

PLANT

ROCKS & MINERALS

SHELL

TREE

VOLCANO &
EARTHQUAKE

WEATHER

THE WORLD AROUND US

BUILDING

CRIME & DETECTION

FARM

FLAG

MEDIA &
COMMUNICATIONS

MONEY

RELIGION

SPY

Future updates and editions will be available online at www.dk.com

DK EYEWITNESS BOOKS

A–Z

DK EYEWITNESS BOOKS

1–110

Future updates and editions will be available online at www.dk.com